<u>~THE RELEASE OF SPIRITUAL KNOWLEDGE~</u>

<u>THE GUIDE:</u>
FOR THOSE LEFT BEHIND
You missed The Rapture!
What You Must Do NEXT

THE ENDTIME WATCHMAN
J. Z. Greene

Send all correspondence to:
Revelation Knowledge Publications
PO Box 2190   St. Louis, Missouri 63032
Or Email: RevelationKnowledgePublication@gmail.com

THE GUIDE FOR THOSE LEFT BEHIND
Copyright © 2020

Cover Designed by: FirstFruits Creative LLC, St. Louis,
MO

Printed by CreateSpace, USA

ISBN 978-1-7338253-1-3

DEDICATION

I dedicate this book to my Lord and Savior, Jesus Christ, the Holy Spirit and the following Saints of God who were placed in my life and were instrumental in guiding my spiritual development into the Will of God for the edification of The Christian Church (Body of Christ)!

Reverend Hampton Minor (In Heaven)
Reverend Frank Moore, Jr. (In Heaven)
Mother Ora Lee Tobias (In Heaven)
Reverend Arthur Daniel (In Heaven)
Mother Annie Williams (In Heaven)
Reverend Louis Brown (In Heaven)
Mother Serata Moore (In Heaven)
Reverend Jodie Nevils, Sr. (In Heaven)
Reverend Clayton Williams (In Heaven)
Brother Watchman Nee (In Heaven)
Brother Smith Wigglesworth (In Heaven)
Brother Clarence Larkin (In Heaven)
Special thanks to:
Phyllis and Charlisha Greene; and Tameka Jones

CONTENTS

Foreword, Introduction, Glossary of Terms

<u>FOREWORD</u>

Approximately 37 years ago my life was given an unhealthy diagnosis by physicians and this man of God, J.Z. Greene, prayed and lead our conversation to believing God for a blessed outcome. The next day he called, with comforting & encouraging words and soon afterward, the x-rays came back without a blemish. Praises became our next conversation and nine months later I became his wife. I would hear elders witness about the Word of God and the Power of God working through my husband/Minister Greene's life as a young man. This was astonishing to me although I knew they had known him from birth. But, one day my Aunt, who only meet him once we got married, spoke to us after hearing him preach a sermon from the Book of Revelation during morning church service, saying she could discern that there was a special anointing upon him and she encouraged him to continue to speak from the Book of Revelation, a book that many Preachers avoid. As the ministry progressed, I saw he was drawn to preach more and more about 'The End Times' and the condition of the people of God. Compassion for the Saints of God was placed heavy upon him, it was evident each time he came before the people to preach or lead a study in the word bible class. Revelation truths and anointing is so applicable and powerful from God thru Minister Greene as he always applies the scriptures. Spiritually the understanding comes forth and the people began to observe the mystery of God's truth. To be a part of this ministry and to personally witness how Minister Greene, sacrifices daily to have study and prayer time with God, and how he consecrates himself to the calling and gifts released to him from God, so that he can fulfil his God appointed assignment.

This book is purposed to help those who were not Raptured with the Saints of God or the Body of Christ. Now, they have an opportunity to look at several things that may have interrupted that purpose that they once anticipated and was not achieved during that time. Also, this book can be inspiring, to many, if read before the Rapture, to make better decisions and choices, and to make sure their desired destination is reached. Oh, how I love seeing my husband/Minister Greene go forth in the work of God! It is also my heart's desire that Minister Greene continues to enjoy his work of the Lord and that Victory in the lives of people will become prominent each time he operates under the anointing of his calling and gifts.

Your Wife ~ Missionary Phyllis Greene

INTRODUCTION

Greetings in the Name of The Lord Jesus Christ, I am The Endtime Watchman, commissioned by God to 'Release Spiritual Knowledge' and blow the trumpet of God to warn those living in this, **THE END OF TIME**! I am commissioned by God to reveal the truth of life that the world is in the midst of a great **SPIRITUAL WARFARE:** A cosmic warfare that is being fought in the invisible realm! This battle could have possibly been going for thousands or even millions of years as we find ourselves infused in the midst of a great controversy between God and Satan!

(<u>Ephesians 6:12</u>) "For we wrestle not against flesh and blood, but against principalities, against powers, against the rulers of the darkness of this world, against spiritual wickedness in high places." (KJV)

The world is now in, what the Bible calls: **'The Great Tribulation'** and many do not realized that humanity wrestles not against flesh and blood; not against each other; our battle is against what cannot be detected by the five senses!!! Our great contest is with various orders of evil spirits (demons), principalities, powers, and rulers of darkness. The **<u>rulers of the darkness of this world</u>**; those evil spirits who rule this world in and through the spiritual darkness; who have already been sentenced by God to eternal damnation! The battle being fought is for "the souls of men, women, boys, and girls" for these evil spirits wish to steal from God, causing many to be damned with them! The Bible calls the forces of Satan **<u>spiritual wickedness in high places</u>**; or, spiritual powers of wickedness, armies of evil spirits in the regions of the air **(See Ephesians 2:2).** The amazing thing about this battle is that it is about to come to an end, we are in the End of Time, we are the last generation! We are the generation that will see the coming of the Lord Jesus Christ who will judge and exterminate all wickedness from the creations of God!

Let it be known since the crucifixion, death, burial and resurrection of the Lord Jesus Christ, He has been gathering the righteous in what the Bible calls **"THE FIRST RESURRECTION,"** taking their righteous spirits to Heaven prior to the wrath to come on the evil ones. I write this book before what is termed, **The Rapture**, has occurred, but Lord has revealed to me that The Rapture of the Christian Church is at hand in which He will suddenly remove or translate the dead in Christ and those living Saints to Heaven in the midst of the Great Tribulation Period!

For the last 7 years, I, preached that Jesus was soon to return warning all who would listen, to **BE READY!** I continuously warned all who would listen, blowing the trumpet without hesitation! On my daily Facebook postings of The Release of Spiritual Knowledge; The Endtime Watchman; The Unified Christian Church; I warned the Saints that we were in the **End of Time** and to be ready! For a full year on my 'Release of Spiritual Knowledge' Radio Program, I warned that the return of The Lord Jesus Christ was imminent, and as in the days of Noah, many scorned the warnings, believing they still had time!

> **(2Peter 3:3-4) Knowing this first, that there shall come in the last days scoffers, walking after their own lusts, And saying, Where is the promise of His coming? for since the fathers fell asleep, all things continue as they were from the beginning of the creation.**

I have been ordered by God to leave this manuscript **THE GUIDE FOR THOSE LEFT BEHIND** as a **biblical guide** to help those not taken away by The Lord Jesus Christ, when He appears in the sky, to gather His Church in The Rapture! Though I know I will be taken, God instructed me to tell those "left behind," **THERE IS STILL HOPE!** Many in these End of Days are professors of Christianity and believed they were in **The Christian Church (The Body of Christ), AND ARE NOT,** having been deceived by the enemy! Many of those who will be left behind have a false perception of <u>what **the true Church** really is, have fallen away from the truth, and do not truly understand that The True Church is a spiritual body, the Mystical Body of Jesus Christ, it is One Church Body, a Called-Out People,</u> not mere material buildings founded by man-made denominational organizations! It seems many, in these end days, do not know that The True Church is not entered by becoming a member or by simply putting your name on a church roll!!

> The Bible says in **(Ephesians 5:6) Let no man deceive you with vain words: for because of these things cometh the wrath of God upon the children of disobedience.**
> The Bible says in **(2Thessalonians 2:3) Let no man deceive you by any means: for that day shall not come, except there comes a falling away first, and that man of sin be revealed, the son of perdition!**

This manuscript was primarily written for you, and if you are reading this book after the event, it means you were not taken in the worldwide disappearance of Christians in what the Christian Church termed as The Rapture! This book is being written as if I am directly talking to you, the individual reading it! If you never heard of the term The Rapture; is an End of Time expression tagged by the Christian Church identifying that the Lord, Jesus Christ, will appear in the sky and raise the dead bodies of true **Christian Believers** who died In-Christ! Then He will gather those who are yet alive, taking them all into Heaven! The event is

Biblically described as part of "THE FIRST RESURRECTION!" The event is predicted in the Bible and described in Paul's First Epistle to the Thessalonians. Here Paul uses **the Greek harpazo (ἁρπάζω),** meaning to **snatch away or seize!** It must be noted that The Rapture is to precede, **The Second Coming of Jesus Christ,** in which He will come to judge the world and to set up His 1000 year reign, this is mentioned in (*Second Thessalonians 1:7-9*):

> **The Rapture - (<u>1 Thessalonians 4:16-17</u>): For the Lord Himself shall descend from Heaven with a shout, with the voice of the Archangel, and with the trump of God: and the dead in Christ shall rise first: Then we which are alive and remain shall be caught up together with them in the clouds, to meet the Lord in the air: and so shall we ever be with the Lord!**

> **The 2nd Coming - (<u>2 Thessalonians 1:7-9</u>) And to you who are troubled rest with us, when the Lord Jesus shall be revealed from Heaven with His mighty angels, In flaming fire taking vengeance on them that know not God, and that obey not the Gospel of our Lord Jesus Christ: Who shall be punished with everlasting destruction from the presence of the Lord, and from the glory of His power.**

Maybe because The Rapture has already happened is the reason you are reading this Book, Praise Be To God! The Holy Spirit of God has instructed me to let you know that **<u>God still loves you and that there is still opportunity for you!</u>** It is my desire in **THE GUIDE FOR THOSE LEFT BEHIND** to help you understand some misconceptions regarding Christianity and to address the numerous deceptions of the enemy that may have possibly caused you to be left behind! I know you may have probing questions you may be debating in your mind, causing you to wonder why Jesus left you behind? I intend to help you to consider several possibilities of what could have happened!!! I will work with you to give you the information you need. If you come to see the reason(s) you were not taken, it will enable you to not repeat the same damning errors giving you an opportunity to revamp your pathway and be saved!

In closing, let me say that as you read **THE GUIDE FOR THOSE LEFT BEHIND,** please have an open mind to examine the things therein! If by some chance **The Rapture** hasn't taken place by the time I release this book, my prayer is that many will read it and be able to know the things they must do to be prepared! I am The Endtime Watchman, sent by God through the Holy Spirit to help those who have been **LEFT BEHIND** to still find their way! I am writing this book while, I, myself, am waiting to be caught up to meet The Lord in the air!

GLOSSARY OF TERMS
(Highlighted Boldly in Text)

Arch Angels – The highest level of angelic beings who stand in the presence of God.
Born – Again - Another term for the Rebirth, accepting Jesus as Savior being Reborn of the Spirit of God
Born of the Spirit - Human beings reborn spiritually by an act of the Spirit of God coming to reside in their spirits.
Born of the Flesh – Human beings who have been born by natural birth the result of the union of a man and woman.
Departed Saints – Christians who have died as believers in the Lord Jesus Christ.
Fallen Angels – Angelic Beings that rebelled against God in the dateless past and fell from their first estate in Heaven.
Form of Godliness – outward appearance of righteousness, a pretense, a outward image, a fake, not real.
God's Plan For The Ages – Is to restore His creations to perfect harmony by removing all evil.
In-Christ – Being spiritually united with Christ, being in Him and Him being in you.
Left Behind – Are those not taken by Jesus Christ to Heaven, in Phase 2 of the First Resurrection in The Rapture.
Living Saints – Christians who are still living and are Believers in the Lord Jesus Christ.
Lucifer - Arch -Angel that lead a rebellion against God in the dateless past whose name was changed to Satan
Plan of Salvation – God's plan to redeem mankind by sending His son to die for our sins.
Resurrection - The ability or power in which Jesus Christ can raise those who have died back to life
Saints – Born Again Believers, children of God, who are Heirs of salvation through Jesus Christ.
Spirit of God – the Holy Spirit, representative of God's Power in action.
Spiritual Enlightenment – Receiving knowledge and understanding about God and His spiritual kingdoms
Spiritual Error – false information, knowledge, activities that can damn the soul for eternity.
Son of David – a name given to the Lord Jesus Christ based on his lineage directly to King David.
Throne of David – Signifies the Divine Throne of God on Earth of which The Lord Jesus Christ will occupy.
The Anointed Cherub that covers – a name given to Lucifer (aka Satan) before his fall from Heaven. He stood in God's presence.
The Body of Christ – The mystical Body of Jesus Christ comprised of true Christian Believers or (Saints) of God
The Church – The mystical body of Christ made up of Born-Again Believers.
The Dateless Past – The period prior to Adam and Eve and prior to the Book of Genesis.
The Day of Judgment -When the wicked will stand before God to be judged.
The Earth Realm – the lowest dimension of light in God's creations. The material and carnal world.
The End of Days or End of the Ages – Same as the End of Time.
The End of Time – The end of Satan's rule over planet earth.
The Father of the Faith – a name for Abraham, who established the faith and how it pleases God.
The First Resurrection – Christ gathering in (3) Phases of all the righteous from Adam up to His 2nd coming.
The Gleanings – The 3rd and last phase of the First Resurrection when Christ will gather the Tribulation Saints
The god of this World – another title for Satan, who rules the earth as a result of stealing it from Adam.
The Gospel – The Word of God as given in the Bible specifically in Matthew, Mark, Luke and John.
The Great and Terrible Day of the Lord – The Second Coming of Jesus Christ.
The Great Tribulation – a 7 year period when God will pour His wrath upon the wicked on earth.
The Harvest - The 2nd phase of the First Resurrection when Christ will gather the Church Saints
The Kingdom of God – the rule of God throughout His created eternal realms.
The Judgement Seat of Christ – The judgement of the righteous by Christ after the Rapture.
The Lake of Fire – The final judgment of the wicked in which their souls shall be cast in eternal fire and brimstone.
The Last Days - The coming up to the end of time given to humanity to rule the earth.
The Physical Realm – the temporal material world, planet earth.
The Material World - 3 dimensional temporal, carnal, world comprising planet earth.
The Millennial Reign of Christ – After the 2nd Coming Christ is to set up a 1000 reign on earth!
The Plan of God – God plan for the Ages of the earth realm, found in the 7 Sealed Book of Revelation.
The Prince of The Powers of the Air – another name for Satan after his fall from Heaven.
The Rapture – When Jesus Christ will appear in the air and gather His true Church.
The Realms of Darkness - the kingdom of Satan including the prison house of Hell or Hades.
The Realms of Light - the Spirit worlds where all is eternity
The Rebirth – Another term for being Born Again, accepting Jesus as Savior being Reborn of the Spirit of God
The Redeemed - Saints of God whose sins have been forgiven by the Risen Christ.
The Release of Spiritual Knowledge – term God gave me for releasing the deeper truths of the Bible.
The Resurrection and the Life – power possessed by Jesus Christ over death and life.
The Righteousness of God – God is holy and only He is pure and righteous.
The Second Coming of Christ – The return of Jesus Christ after the Great Tribulation.
The Second Death – Eternal separation of the soul or spirit from God by being cast into the Lake of Fire.
The Second Resurrection – is when all the wicked will be raised to stand before God and judged.
The Spirit of Christ – The Spirit or Christ is the Holy Spirit through which He indwells His people.
The Spirit World – the eternal worlds and dimensions of God
The Time of Jacob's Trouble – Refers to The Great Tribulation period when Israel (Jacob) will be tested.
The Time of Trouble - refers to the Great Tribulation period when the wicked will suffer great perils.
The Time Realm – the physical, material, carnal, temporal world, which is the lowest level of God creation(s).
The Wilderness of the People – the suffering of the Children of Israel during Moses times and in the end of time.

CHRONOLOGICAL ORDER OF
THE NEW TESTAMENT DISPENSATIONAL WORK OF
THE LORD JESUS CHRIST
AS HE MINISTERS THE FIRST RESURRECTION

(The 1st Resurrection is the gathering of Christ of all the righteous)- The Birth
of Christ.
- The Earthly Ministry of Christ.
- The Crucifixion & Physical Death of Christ.
- The Burial of Christ.
- The Descent of The Spirit of Christ into Hades (Hell)T.
- The Defeat of Death & Hell by Christ.
Christ preaches to the spirits (from Adam) in Hell.
- The Rising from the Dead of Christ.
TIMELINE - (2000 years ago).

|

- The Resurrection of the Captives in Hell (THE FIRSTFRUITS).

|

- The Ascension of Christ.
- The Sending of the Holy Ghost by Christ to Believers.
- The Ministry of Christ as High Priest intercessor for mankind.
- The Work of Christ through The Church (As The Head).
TIMELINE - (1st 3 ½ years of The Great Tribulation).

⊥

- The Resurrection or Rapture of the Church by Christ (THE HARVEST.)

|

TIMELINE – (Last 3 ½ years of The Great Tribulation).

|

- The Resurrection of the Tribulation Saints (THE GLEANINGS).

|

TIMELINE – (At the end of - The Great Tribulation).
- The Second Coming of Christ.
- The 1000 Millennial Year Reign of Christ.

|

TIMELINE – (At the end of – The 1000 year Reign of Christ).
- The Resurrection of the Wicked Dead by Christ.
- The Great White Throne Judgment of God.
- The Casting of All the Wicked in The Lake of Fire.
- Christ turning the Kingdom over to GOD The Father.

=================================
~THE RELEASE OF SPIRITUAL KNOWLEDGE~
THE GUIDE FOR THOSE LEFT BEHIND
You Missed the Rapture! What You Must Do NEXT
=================================

CHAPTER 1
THE WAR BETWEEN GOD AND SATAN

WHAT THIS CHAPTER IS ABOUT
I WISH TO TAKE YOU BACK IN THE DATELESS PAST THAT YOU MAY SEE AND
UNDERSTAND WHY THE PLANET IS NOW IN THE GREAT TRIBULATION! THE
TIME THE WORLD IS IN IS A TIME OF HORRIFIC JUDGMENT THAT HAS NEVER
BEEN SINCE CREATION OF THE EARTH! STRANGE THINGS ARE HAPPENING
BECAUSE THE CAUSE OF IT ALL IS A SUPERNATURAL WAR THAT IS BEING WAGED
BY INVISIBLE EVIL FORCES WHO REBELLED AGAINST THE ALMIGHTY GOD! YES,
THE PLANET AND ITS INHABITANTS ARE IN THE MIDDLE OF AN AGE-OLD
CONFLICT! YOU NEED TO UNDERSTAND HOW YOU, AN ETERNAL SPIRIT IN A
PHYSICAL BODY, BECAME IMMERSED IN THE CONFLICT! IT'S NECESSARY FOR
YOU TO COMPREHEND THE CAUSE OF IT ALL! LET US GO BACK IN THE
DATELESS PAST AND SEE!

***(Hosea 4:6)** My people are destroyed for lack of knowledge:
because thou hast rejected knowledge, I will also reject thee, that
thou shalt be no priest to me: seeing thou hast forgotten the law
of thy God, I will also forget thy children.*

Now that the true Christian Church has been removed by
Christ, it is necessary for you to be educated in some of the things
pertaining to God that evidently you did not understand! Now
listen, if it would help you, if you were one of those professing
Christianity and was deceived by Satan, **know that Jesus still
loves you and has made a way for you** if you are willing to step
into it!   This kind of conversation is necessary for your **spiritual
enlightenment** and is essential for us to lay a spiritual foundation
to build on. I will only convey to you what you need as guided by
the Holy Spirit. You cannot eat meat, so I must feed you with milk
(1Corinthians 3:2)!   I will not go into an expanded presentation
of biblical exposition but will give what will enable you to
understand versus, be confused! By exposing you to **The Release**

of Spiritual Knowledge it should fortify you to make the hard decisions you will have to make, decisions you must make to avoid eternal damnation in the Lake of Fire!   So, let us begin my Brother or Sister**!**

The world is an evil place and the root of all evil in the world is engineered by invisible spiritual evil forces in the heavenlies that are in rebellion against God! Without going into an extended explanation, my intent is to give you a glimpse into this rebellion. **The Earth Realm** or the material world was brought into existence by **The Plan of God** to deal with a disturbance that He knew would occur in His creation!   In God's Plan, Jesus was to come and die on the cross! To understand this will further enable you to see why the world is now going through **Great Tribulation** at this, **The End of Time!** God has commissioned me to provide a Release of Spiritual Knowledge and there is so much I can impart, but I just need to give insight into **God's Plan for The Ages**! The creations of God are all spiritual eternal realms of Glory except The Earth Realm which is a material, temporal, and restricted plane, created by God for a specific reason! You need to understand this knowledge because you can never know the future if you do not understand what has happened in the past! It is absolutely necessary for me to give you a glimpse of the past so that you may understand why the world is saturated with evil and why it is now standing at The End of Time and about to be judged by God!

First, I wish to open you up to the great spiritual deceptions that exist, for what you think you see is not what is, and what you think you know is not reality.   Then we will look at why you are now facing Great Tribulation with the wicked, having missed **The Rapture** of the Christian Church! Think about this statement, when men and women abuse God's goodness by increasingly sinning against Him even though He still blesses them, it is a tragedy that they seem to become more wicked as they become more privileged and more prosperous! It seems men and women do not understand that not honoring God manifest the sure mark of degeneration upon themselves and leads to approaching destruction! Because of the prosperity and privilege of those in these End Days many have become victims of the Wrath to Come!

(A)   <u>A GLIMPSE INTO THE DATELESS PAST</u>

Since you are reading this book, I am going to assume you believe in the reality of God, the Creator of all that exists! I, for clarity purposes, wish to say that God is One and is the source of all Life, The Supreme Being! All is sustained by His Almighty Power! His Glory fills and filters down throughout all His created realms, worlds, dimensions, dominions, and gives life to all! He is God, there is no other! He sits outside of His creation(s) and His Glory or Light is Life!!! We cannot imagine the magnitude of His power for it has no limits! He is eternal, everlasting to everlasting! The expansion of His created worlds is limitless – and beyond our imagination! So, with that said, let us investigate **The Dateless Past!**

In the dateless past, meaning before God made Adam and Eve the entire Creation(s) of God was in harmony with God will! It is a known fact that the Creation of God is comprised of untold dimensions, worlds, spheres, comprised of eternal spiritual beings, all created by God and for God! I believe and must stress to you that the limitations of The Time Realm, or for clarity purposes, The Physical or Material Realm, did not exist in the dateless past and the complete creation(s) of God was a **Spiritual Realm,** eternal and never-ending with no death, pain, suffering, sorrow, hatred, strife, you get the picture! In the Dateless Past the sons of God (spiritual and eternal Angelic beings), ruled the planets and the stars and all reported to God periodically regarding their spheres of dominion!

__(John 1:6)__ Now there was a day when the sons of God came to present themselves before the LORD, and Satan came also among them.

It is a fact the highest-ranking angels are Arch-Angels! Because they are **Arch-Angels**, they have direct access to **The Throne of God,** and they can stand in the highest Realm or highest Heaven in the presence of God!   **Lucifer** was the highest-ranking arch-angel in the creation of God, ruler of planet Earth in the dateless past, and was recognized as the most gifted, most beautiful, and most influential Angelic Being in eternity past! Lucifer was called the **Anointed Cherub That Covers,** meaning, he was a Protector and Guardian of the Throne of God! He was perfect in all his ways until iniquity was found in him **(Ezekiel 28:15)!** It was Lucifer, in the dateless past, who lead, and convinced numerous Angelic Beings to participate in a sin rebellion against God in order to free themselves from God's rule! This rebellion caused Lucifer and these conspirators, after their defeat, to be stripped of their power, position, dominion, and authority! For God has ALL POWER! After being stripped, they were cast out of the higher realms of Glory and isolated in the lower realms of creation, just above Planet Earth!   Yes, Planet Earth, which I forestated, was Lucifer's prior ruling planet after rebellion against God, was transformed into the lowest realm or dimension in the creation(s) of God.   It was destroyed and covered with water and transformed into a 3-dimensional world, becoming a physical place and the Light of God's Glory that once shined upon it, was diminished (dimmed)!   The Earth Lucifer once ruled, became a desolated planet, destroyed, a wasteland!   The fallen Lucifer's name was changed to **Satan,** and now he became **the prince of the powers of the air** (the prince of the fallen angels), **the god of this world** (a fallen and temporal world**),** the god of the world's evil systems, because he continues to escalate a progressive sin rebellion against the Most High! Because Lucifer had fallen, The Earth also was changed becoming a place with parameters, limitations, destructive principles that could destroy, and confinement! In this Earth Realm there also are things that do not exist in the spiritual realms; specifically: restricted mobility, lack, sickness, disease, hatred, conflict, deterioration, death, pain, suffering, and sorrow; you get the picture! But God in His wisdom had a plan and a purpose for lowering the planet to a **Time Realm,** creating a place to punish all the wicked, as you will see!

(B) <u>**THE ETERNITY OF OUR SPIRITS**</u>

There is a conflict between God and Satan over the spirits of men, women, boys, and girls. Satan is attempting to damn the spirits of humanity whereas God is attempting to deliver us from damnation! I am going to cut through the chase with you regarding who we are! We are eternal spirits created by God that are housed in physical bodies so that we can experience life in what is called the physical plain or physical realm, The Earth Realm! I forestated that Planet Earth is unique in the creations of God for it is a material, physical, carnal and 3-dimensional world! So, being created by God as eternal spirits, why would He expose our spirits to this physical realm? Get this: He proceeded to birth us into this world enabling us to access this carnal, material dimension, exposing us into an environment whose history was unknown! God wanted to test us by subjecting us to a changeable environment! Think about it, if you were born in pure light and you were composed of light, how could you determine who you are – from the light that you were saturated in? All of God's created beings must be tested to find out who and what they are!!!

So, God making man in His image and likeness, still had to test this new form of eternal being. That is right, consider that Adam and Eve did not know that an invisible evil entity was present! Now you should understand that you will never die, only your body dies, but you, being an **eternal spirit**, will live forever! So when you look at someone that has died, laying in a casket, understand that they really did not die, only the physical body died, the person is an eternal spirit and lives on, and that person's spirit simply separated out of the physical body, the house it was in, and was transported into another dimension, **The Spirit Realm**! Let me give you a few scriptures to clarity this information!

Notice that Jesus always associated what we think of as death as sleep, for example:

.   1) The story of Lazarus   *(John 11:11) These things said He: and after that He saith unto them, Our friend Lazarus sleepeth; but I go, that I may awake him out of sleep.*

2)   What Jesus said about the maiden that was considered dead in *(Matthew 9:24) He said unto them, give place: for the maid is not dead, but sleepeth. And they laughed Him to scorn.*

3)   What happened with the damsel in *(Mark 5:39) And when He was come in, He saith unto them, why make ye this ado, and weep? The damsel is not dead, but sleepeth.*

4)   Even Satan knew that Adam and Eve were eternal spirits in bodies, did he not tell Eve in *(Genesis 3:4) And the serpent said unto the woman, Ye shall not surely die:*

In other words, your body will die but you, the real you, which is eternal, will not die! So, being eternal spirits, we are all important to God because we will never die or cease to exist, that is why God cares about our eternal destination, and if we want eternity in Heaven or in Glory we must cooperate with God to get back there!

(C)   <u>GOD KNEW SATAN WOULD TEMPT ADAM WHEN HE MADE HIM</u>

Now that you have a clearer glimpse of the past you are probably wondering why GOD created man and put him in the middle of this great spiritual warfare that was happening between Himself and Satan. Another question you may be asking is; if

GOD knows all things, why did He allow Satan to progress his evil plans? I want you to understand that GOD knew that Lucifer and a third of the angelic host would fall, causing a sin rebellion in His creation! When He created Lucifer, GOD knew what Lucifer would do, for GOD knows the past, present and future! Nothing surprises GOD, that's why He is GOD, The Almighty! With that said, from the foundation of the world, GOD had a plan to deal with the rebellion. That plan was hidden in Him and manifested according to GOD'S own will and in GOD'S designated time! As forestated, GOD had diminished the earth to a carnal world for a reason, which was not just to create a new race of beings, but also to provide the parameters needed to sentence Satan and the fallen angels to eternal punishment! The judgment required on Satan and the fallen angels did not exist in the realms of light in eternal glory, so the diminishing changes brought on the earth realm, provided what God required to eradicate evil for all eternity! Now, let's look at it this way, yes, God knew that man would fall; but God in His wisdom wanted to create a unique race of spiritual beings <u>that would be like Him</u>! Yes, He made mankind in His image and after His likeness and placed them in The Garden of Eden, giving them dominion over Lucifer's previous ruling planet, knowing that Satan was lurking!

> **_(Genesis 1:26-27)_** **_And God said, Let Us make man in Our image, after Our likeness: and let them have dominion over the fish of the sea, and over the fowl of the air, and over the cattle, and over all the earth, and over every creeping thing that creepeth upon the earth. So, God created man in His own image, in the image of God created He him; male and female created He them._**

Understand that the Almighty God gives all his creatures free will to choose! Man had to be tested to determine if his self-will was to obey to God, and what better way to test him than to use **Lucifer and the Fallen Angel**s, to do so? It is obvious that even Lucifer and the fallen angels had the ability of free will and chose on their own to rebel against God and the Kingdom of Heaven!

They were not automated beings, but they had a choice and they chose rebellion and attempted to overthrow God! I believe, by the Holy Spirit in The Release of Spiritual Knowledge that God tests all His beings, regardless, and that testing determines their existence in **The Realms of Light** or the dimensions of **The Spirit World.** From Adam to Christ, they were tested to obedience: some passed the test, and some failed the test! Jesus was tested by Satan; Job felt he was being tested by God; Joseph was tested because he was in a foreign place and it was hard for him; Jonah was tested because he didn't want to obey God and go to Nineveh, did he not end up inside a whale; Eve was tested by Satan and gave in; Adam was tested by Satan through Eve and disobeyed God; Noah was tested by God to have faith to build the ark; Abraham and Sarah were tested to believe that God would give them a child; Abraham was tested when God asked him to sacrifice his son; Mary was tested when God chose her to have a baby without having ever been with a man; Joseph was tested when God told him to believe that Mary had not cheated on him; **AND IN THIS WORLD YOU HAVE BEEN TESTED TO SEE IF YOU WOULD REMAIN FAITHFUL TO GOD**! God uses trials, temptations, persecution and afflictions to test His Children, that is a fact!

> ***(1Corinthians 10:13)*** *There hath no temptation taken you but such as is common to man: but God is faithful, who will not suffer you to be tempted above that ye are able; but will with the temptation also make a way to escape, that ye may be able to bear it.*

God desires for us all to choose to obey Him, to be faithful to His will; He wants us to trust His Word for our lives, He is our Creator! So, what I am saying to you is; in this world, this physical realm, you are tested to see if you will be worthy to enter the eternal Realms of Light, the spiritual realms of joy and peace, to live in the presence of God for all eternity and not in **The Realms of Darkness** and damnation!! Those that were worthy were taken in The Rapture, and those that were not, were left behind! So, the answer is: yes, God knew when He created Adam and Eve what would happen in the Garden, but in God's Plan, He would redeem man through Jesus Christ, and any who choose to obey and serve Him! Praise God, it is so great of a plan, that through Jesus Christ, God would redeem mankind and destroy Satan and his fallen angels, WHAT **A MIGHTY GOD!**

CHAPTER 2
GOD'S PENDING JUDGMENT OF THE WICKED

WHAT THIS CHAPTER IS ABOUT
IN CHAPTER 1 THE CONFLICT WAS REVEALED AND THE REASON MANKIND WAS INFUSED IN IT! IN THIS CHAPTER I WISH TO ALLUDE TO THE CAUSE OF THE GREAT TRIBULATION THE WORLD IS NOW IN! IT IS THE JUDGMENT OF GOD AGAINST SATAN AND THE FALLEN ANGELS: FOR THEIR TIME OF INDEPENDENCE IS UP! WHAT IS NOW TAKING PLACE ON PLANET EARTH ARE THE BIRTH PANGS THAT WILL PROGRESS TO INTRODUCE THE KING OF GLORY, THE LORD JESUS CHRIST AND REMOVE THE ENEMIES OF GOD FOREVER! LET US CONSIDER THE SENTENCE ALL THE WICKED SHALL SUFFER!

(A) A HISTORICAL AND REALISTIC LOOK AT WHAT IS ABOUT TO OCCUR

It is required that you believe that Satan is real and the entire history of planet earth is centered around his past and current rebellion against God! As an arch-angel that once stood in the presence of God in the highest Heaven, he is beyond contempt having had direct access to the **Throne of God!** As forestated, his fall from grace came as he and a third of the angels of Heaven conceived a ridiculous plot and an even more preposterous attempt to overthrow the **Kingdom of God!** It is unknown how long ago in time this foolish scheme happened, but what is known is that they are approaching their coming eternal damnation in the **Lake of Fire** which God has ordained for their eternal punishment! What is sad is that wicked men and women, boys and girls who have been deceived by Satan and the forces of evil to also rebel against God, will share in their condemnation! Let us look briefly at what the Bible illustrates that Jesus, The Father' administrator, will do regarding the coming judgment of the wicked.

(B) <u>THE COMING JUDGEMENT OF THE WICKED</u>

<u>(Matthew 25:41)</u> Then shall He say also unto them on the left hand, Depart from me, ye cursed, into everlasting fire, prepared for the devil and his angels:

To familiarize you, the reader, with some the terms being used, please understand that Jesus is coming back (2) times, the first time He is to appear in the air (heavens) and gather those who are a part of His true Church in a coming called "**The Rapture!**" At the time I was writing this book I believed "The Rapture" was very close to occurring! When I speak of **The Second Coming of Christ,** I am talking about the final coming of Christ which will take place after **The Great Tribulation**! Christ will descend from Heaven and touch down on the Mount of Olives in Jerusalem with the Raptured Saints and the armies of Heaven and set up the **Millennial Reign of Christ** or 1000-year kingdom; this will happen at The Second Coming of Christ!

It is after The Second Coming of Christ, and after the Millennial Reign of Christ when Jesus will say to the wicked, "Depart from me, ye cursed, into everlasting fire!" Those that have sought the Lord on earth shall be with Him forever **(1Thessalonians 4:17***).* Those who have turned away from The Lord and the salvation He offers shall be turned away from Him forever. The punishment is everlasting banishment from His presence **(2Thessalonians 1:9).** Ye are cursed! Under the Jewish law, anything irretrievably condemned and devoted to death was called **accursed (Deuteronomy 13:17).** Here, Jesus uses the same term and applies it to the wicked, a sentence of eternal death! As taught in Chapter 1 of **The Guide to Those Left Behind,** your spirit cannot die, but your spirit can be banished from God who is the source of life! If banished, your spirit can never be allowed to house a body again, whether it's a physical body or spiritual body. Your spirit becomes bodiless, banished from God for eternity in the flames of eternal fire and brimstone, never being allowed to experience the joys of life again! And where will the punishment be applied? Into **Everlasting Fire,** prepared for the devil and his angels. Fire is probably used, as in many other places in the scripture, to illustrate the bitterness of the punishment of the wicked. Note: (1) it is everlasting and (2) it was not prepared for mankind, but for the devil and his angels! Those who choose to associate and align themselves with Satan, will as the result, share the damnable sentence of Satan and the fallen angels!

(C) LET'S TAKE A GLIMPSE OF HOW SATAN & HIS FORCES SHALL COME TO THEIR END

> ***(Revelation 12:9) And the great dragon was cast out, that old serpent, called the Devil, and Satan, which deceives the whole world: he was cast out into the earth, and his angels were cast out with him!***

The Book of Revelation illustrates a glimpse of the fact that in The End Of Time, which is now, Satan and his evil forces, the fallen angels, will be cast out of Heaven or the heavenlies (the air). I believe this has already happened because the true Christian Church has been Raptured. And since Satan and the fallen angels have been cast out of the heavenlies and cast down into the earth this means that he knows his time is short! The dragon in Heaven is thought by many to mean the devil enthroned in the chief place of power; the dragon on earth, to mean the devil cast out of that place, but still, waging an active warfare against those believing in Jesus and anyone that has an allegiance to God!

(1)
THOUGH CAST OUT OF HEAVEN THE REBELLION CONTINUES

> ***(Revelation 12:13-14) says: And when the dragon saw that he was cast unto the earth, he persecuted the woman (the Jews) which brought forth the man child. And to the woman were given two wings of a great eagle, that she might fly into the wilderness, into her place, where she is nourished for a time, and times, and half a time, from the face of the serpent.***

Satan and his evil forces are continuing their rebellion against God by attacking the seed of Christ (the Jews) and those who choose to obey God (Tribulation Saints)! Understand that whoever may be the instruments of persecuting the people of God, Satan is their leader; they are his servants, and are doing his work. So, it is of upmost importance for you to determine who your allegiance will be to, will it be God or to man (Anti-Christ) during this critical period in which you find yourself! **And though the way may seem hard, understand that you still have hope, though you have been left behind**!

(2)
ONLY THE RETURN OF JESUS WILL STOP SATAN FROM TEMPTING MANKIND

During this tribulation period that the world is now going through, Satan and his forces of evil are still loosed and are still deceiving those who are in the world. While this world suffers through The Great Tribulation, Satan's activities will not be destroyed immediately but he will increase his activities against mankind because he knows his time is short. At the end of The Great Tribulation when Jesus Christ returns at His Second Coming, Satan will be bound for 1000 years and will not have the ability to tempt mankind to do evil during that 1000-year period.

(3)
SATAN WILL BE BOUND IN THE BOTTOMLESS PIT FOR 1000 YEARS

> *(Revelation 20:1-2) And I saw an angel come down from heaven, having the key of the bottomless pit and a great chain in his hand. And he laid hold on the dragon, that old serpent, which is the Devil, and Satan, and bound him a thousand years, and cast him into the bottomless pit, and shut him up, and set a seal upon him, that he should deceive the nations no more, till the thousand years should be fulfilled: and after that he must be loosed a little season.*

When Jesus comes back at The Second Coming, He will send an Angel of God and He shall lay hold on the dragon (Satan), and bind him a thousand years, chaining him for 1000 years as ordered by The Word of God. When this happens, the triumph of the righteousness of the Gospel takes such hold of the hearts of men, they will rejoice that Satan loses his powers over them! We can easily see how this is accomplished by what takes place under our own eyes. A man may be drunken and lawless, but if he repents under the influence of the Gospel, it causes him to cease serving Satan and the devil loses his power over that man. When that period shall come for which the saints of all ages have wistfully looked, when the laws of God shall be written upon every heart, then Satan, bound with a chain, shall be deprived of influence on the earth. Here is shown in scripture how Satan is restrained by Christ, by His Almighty Power, shall keep the devil from deceiving mankind as he has done since the creation of Adam! The power of Christ is used to put a stop to the power of Satan's power, sealing and binding him in the bottomless pit! During this time of Christ's 1000-year reign, the world shall have a time of peace and prosperity, but understand, all her trials are not yet over!

(4)
<u>SATAN IS THEN LOOSED, AND CONTINUES TO DECEIVE MANKIND</u>

(Revelation 20:7-8) **And when the thousand years are expired, Satan shall be loosed out of his prison, And shall go out to deceive the nations which are in the four quarters of the earth, Gog and Magog, to gather them together to battle: the number of whom is as the sand of the sea.**

At the end of the 1000 year reign of Christ, Satan is let loose, and he again begins deceiving the nations, and stirring them up to make war with the Saints and Servants of God (those who have been saved during the 1000 year reign). I say again, when the thousand years are expired, Satan shall be loosed. The earth shall have had its golden age, but it shall not last forever. Satan shall, when 1000 years have rolled away, be loosed! From some cause, that is wrapped in the darkness of the future, righteousness shall wane; wickedness shall revive; the great adversary shall in part, regain his influence over many in humanity. But it is comforting to know that his triumph will be short. He shall be loosed only for a little season **(Revelation 20:3).** If only the servants and ministers of Christ were as active and persevering in doing good, as their enemies are in doing mischief, many would have understood the wiles that Satan and his forces of evil and how they were working in the world. But God will fight this last and decisive battle for His people, that the victory may be complete, and the glory be to Himself!

(5)
<u>SATAN & THE FORCES OF EVIL ARE CAST INTO THE LAKE OF FIRE</u>

(Revelation 20:10) And the devil that deceived them was cast into the lake of fire and brimstone, where the beast and the false prophet are, and shall be tormented day and night for ever and ever.

Now, I want to summarize for you the biography of Lucifer (Satan) and his judgment along with the fallen angels and the wicked, that you may get a clear picture! I am giving you a look in the past and the future of all the wicked for you to understand the importance of the horrific world events occurring all around, for you are in the GREAT TRIBULATION! Let's look again at a summary of Satan, this fearful being, apparently created as one of the Cherubim anointed for a position of great authority, perhaps over the primitive creation, **(See Ezekiel 28:11-15).** He fell through pride **(See Isaiah 14:12-14)** and voiced his will against the Will of The Almighty God! That act marks the introduction of sin into the creations of God.   Yes, he was cast out of Heaven **(See Luke 10:18)** and made earth and air the location of his tireless activity **(See Ephesians 2:2; 1Pe 5:8).** After the creation of man, he entered the serpent. **(See Genesis 3:1)** and, beguiling Eve by his subtilty, secured the downfall of Adam and through him, the downfall of the entire human race, bringing the seed of sin into the world of men **(See Romans 5:12-14).**   In the Adamic Covenant **(See Genesis 3:14),** God promised the ultimate destruction of Satan through the seed of the woman. Then Satan began his long warfare against the work of God on behalf of humanity, which continues! The present world-system **(See Revelation 13:8)** is organized by Satan and the forces of evil upon the principles of greed, selfishness, ambition, and sinful pleasure, are all is his work and was the bribe which he offered to Adam, Eve & Christ **(See**

Matthew 4:8-9). Of that world-system he is prince **(See John 14:30; 16:11)** and god **(See 2Corinthians 4:4).** As prince of the power of the air **(See Ephesians 2:2)** he is at the head of a vast host of demons (which are disembodied evil spirits which I believe are the offspring of the fallen angels) **(See Matthew 7:22)!** To him, under God, was committed upon earth the power of death, because of sin, for the wages of sin is death **(See Hebrews 2:14).** Though Satan (then Lucifer) was cast out of heaven, he still has access to God as the accuser of the Brethren **(See Revelation 12:10)** and is permitted certain power to sift or test those who are self-confident and carnal among Believers **(See Job 1:6-11; Luke 22:31-32; 1Corinthians 5:5; 1Timothy 1:20).** Satan has strictly permissive (you must allow)and limited power, and Believers so sifted are kept in faith through the advocacy of Christ **(See Luke 22:31-32) & (1John 2:1).** At the withdrawal of the Body of Christ, The Church, when The Rapture took place, Satan's privilege of access to God as accuser was terminated **(See Revelation 12:7-12).** At the return of Christ in Glory or at **The Second Coming of Christ**, Satan will be bound for one thousand years **(See Revelation 20:2)** after which he will be loosed for a little season **(See Revelation 20:3,7-8)** and will become the head of a final attempt to overthrow The Kingdom of God. Defeated in this, he will be finally cast into The Lake of Fire, along with the angels who rebelled with him; and demonic spirits, this is their final doom. The notion that he reigns in hell is not illustrated by scripture and, is not biblical. He is prince of this present world-system but will be tormented in The Lake of Fire!

    <u>And the devil that deceived them was cast into The Lake of Fire</u>. Because this is an important term I want to clarify more clearly what it is: The Lake of Fire is; the place prepared for the devil and those who cooperate with him in opposing the cause of Christ **(See Matthew 25:41).** So it is relevant for you to see that the flesh is naturally wicked and, when enticed by the malignancy and power of Satan, humanity can be prone to oppose God, specially is Satan is not restrained, and men are left without divine grace! . What you are amidst and what you are seeing is Satan's last battle! The Christian Church has been raptured by Christ! **<u>Now</u>**

<u>Satan is attacking and trying to mislead those who still have a hope in Christ</u>!   His time of judgment has come! The great deceiver is not cast into the bottomless pit yet. The Lake of Fire is opened, and we discover there the beast and the false prophet, but they have gone where none ever return. There the devil will be cast in and locked up to abide with his allies in wickedness forever! I hope and pray this clarifies in your mind how the enemy of your soul is operating! What you are facing is beyond all carnal logic and demands that you operate by faith in God and in His Word. In order to avoid the coming eternal destruction I am asking you to obey what I am showing you in God's Word, **<u>though you missed The Rapture, God has still allowed one last path for you and others who obey, a chance to avoid the sentence of the wicked!</u>**   Let's continue.

CHAPTER 3
WE ARE IN THE GREAT TRIBULATION

WHAT THIS CHAPTER IS ABOUT
IN CHAPTER 2 IT WAS REVEALED THE CONFLICT RESULTED IN THE
VERDICT OF GOD UPON SATAN AND WICKED HUMANITY! IN THIS
CHAPTER, I WISH TO VALIDATE IN YOUR MIND THAT THE EARTH IS IN
THE TIME OF THE GREAT TRIBULATION WHICH MARKS, THE END OF
TIME, THE END OF THE AGE OF THE GENTILES, OR NON GOD
BELIEVING PEOPLE. IT IS THE TIME IN WHICH CHRIST SHALL
RETURN, AND WE SEE THE END OF THE DISPENSATION OF GRACE! IT
IS A TIME OF TROUBLE, NEVER BEFORE SEEN SINCE THE BEGINNING
OF TIME!

A BIBLICAL LOOK AT THE TERM GREAT TRIBULATION AND WHAT IT MEANS

I have been using the term **The Great Tribulation** and I
think I should give you a very clear understanding of what the term
means! The scriptures speak of a Great Tribulation that is to
come on the Earth during the time **The Church** is on Earth, and
even after The Church is removed from the earth, it will continue
to play out! Planet Earth is now in the period in the plan of God
called **The Great Tribulation,** a period of (7) years! And since I
believe the Rapture of the Church took place in the middle of The
Great Tribulation it would mean that there are three and a half (3
½) years left before the 2nd coming of the Lord Jesus Christ! The
last 3 ½ years will be the most horrifying, catastrophic period the
earth has ever experienced!   Starting in Chapter 8 of The Book of
Revelation this period commences with the breaking of what the
Bible calls the 7th Seal, which comprises the judgments of God
upon the wicked!   The breaking of **The 7th Seal** is followed or
highlighted by **The 7 Trumpets and The 7 Vials;** which are
judgements that will be poured out upon the earth that will be so
devastating that humans will desire to die and death will flee from
them!

> ***(Revelation 9:6)*** *And in those days shall men seek death, and shall not find it; and shall desire to die, and death shall flee from them.*

It is relevant for you to understand that The Great Tribulation has something also to do with **The Jewish People** and is a judgment in which they must **Pass Under The Rod (See Ezekiel 20:34-38),** and in which God will cast Israel into His **Melting Pot (See Ezekiel 22:19-22)** where they are to be refined as **gold is refined.** God is sending Israel through The Great Tribulation to fit them to again be called His chosen people!   Because the Great Tribulation marks the end of **The Gentiles** or (the unsaved masses and their rule over the earth), they will be affected by the Great Tribulation also. Since the Church has been Raptured or caught up, it will not have to suffer the wrath portion of The Great Tribulation period or the last 3 ½ year!

Jesus in His Olivet Discourse uttered on the Mount of Olives before His crucifixion that The Great Tribulation was coming upon the planet!   I have already told you that this event is a sign that the **End of the Ages** and the judgment of all evil has come! Not only did Jesus Himself reveal The Great Tribulation, but so did the Prophets: Daniel, Jeremiah, and Ezekiel! Let's study in this chapter what Jesus and the great Prophets had to say about this event that the earth is now in!

(A) <u>JESUS FORETOLD THE GREAT TRIBULATION</u>

In the Book of Matthew Jesus said: ***(Matthew 24:21-22)*** *For then shall be Great Tribulation, such as was not since the beginning of the world to this time, no, nor ever shall be.· And except those days should be shortened, there should no flesh be saved: but for the elect's sake those days shall be shortened.*

Jesus defined this time of The Great Tribulation as a time of world judgement, the judgment of wickedness of humanity and the wicked ones, Satan and the fallen angels!   Jesus knew the Church would be caught up before that **Great and Terrible Day of the Lord** when the wrath of God would be poured out on wicked inhabitants of the earth! Jesus describe The Great Tribulation by saying, then shall be great tribulation, or great distress! Millions will be slain, and multitudes will be brought into perpetual bondage, and hordes will perish by famine, pestilence, and cruel treatment! The period will be so horrific that Jesus says except those days, meaning days of distress, be shortened, no flesh will be able to survive!   What He is literary saying is that all flesh will perish if God does not shorten or limit the time of the Great Tribulation! But for the Elect's sake; those whom God had chosen to be His people (Israel), the days of The Great Tribulation are limited!

(B) THE PROPHET DANIEL FORETOLD THE GREAT TRIBULATION

In the Bible, it is a time termed by the Prophet Daniel as **A Time of Trouble** defining the refining of the Jewish people; the Prophet Daniel was seeing The Great Tribulation!

In the Book of Daniel, the prophet said in*: (Daniel 12:1) And at that time shall Michael stand up, the great prince which standeth for the children of thy people: and there shall be a Time of Trouble, such as never was since there was a nation even to that same time: and at that time thy people shall be delivered, every one that shall be found written in the book.*

At Israel's time of trouble, the Arch-Angel Michael, shall stand up for the working out of Israel's eternal salvation!   Have we all not needed the divine help of angels in our journey through this evil world?   In this time of tribulation, Jesus, The Son of God shall be manifested to destroy the works of the devil!   Before Christ appears at His Second Coming, He will recompense Great Tribulation to those that trouble His people!   There shall be a time of trouble threatening all that are in the world, as was not since the beginning of the world to that time, a time of trouble as never was, to all those whom Michael our Prince stands against! The Book of Daniel goes on to say there will be a resurrection of those whose bodies sleep in dust, a general resurrection at the Last Day, saying, the multitude of those that sleep in the dust shall awaken!! Some shall be awakened to life and some shall be awakened to face eternal damnation in the Lake of Fire!

> *(Daniel 12:2)* **And many of them that sleep in the dust of the earth shall awake, some to everlasting life, and some to shame and everlasting contempt.**

(C) THE PROPHET JEREMIAH FORETOLD OF THE GREAT TRIBULATION

The Great Tribulation is referred to by Old Testament Prophet Jeremiah as, **The Time of Jacob's Trouble,** in:

> *(Jeremiah 30: 4-7)* **And these are the words that the LORD spake concerning Israel and concerning Judah. For thus saith the LORD, we have heard a voice of trembling, of fear, and not of peace. Ask ye now, and see whether a man doth travail with child? Wherefore do I see every man with his hands on his loins, as a woman in travail, and all faces are turned into paleness? Alas! for that day is great, so that none is like it: it is even The Time of Jacob's Trouble; but he shall be saved out of it.**

The Time of Jacob's Trouble, is clarified in the above scripture and compared with the previous scripture (**Daniel 12:1**) which I just explained.   The great deliverances of God's church have been achieved in troublous times, she has been raptured out of The Great Tribulation, but Israel is left in it. Jeremiah wrote what God had spoken to him. The very words are such as the Holy Ghost teaches. These are the words God ordered to be written; and He promises to bring forth what is written!   I, **The Endtime Watchman,** must also write a description of the trouble the world is now in, knowing that many are likely to not anticipate the magnitude of the troubles that lie ahead!   **A happy end can be put to these calamities to those that will hear and are willing to obey!** Though the afflictions of the Church may have lasted long, they did not last always for The Church has been raptured out of **T**he Great Tribulation!   And the seed that brought Christ into the world, The Jews, are now going through Great Tribulation, and the whole world will seem to stand against them!   But the Jews also shall be rescued and restored again by God, according to His promises to Abraham, Isaac, and Jacob!   They, The Jews, shall obey, and call upon the Messiah, The Christ, the Son of David, their King!   The deliverance of The Jews, in this, the End of Time from its tormentors, will be the outcome of The Great Tribulation, as pointed out in the prophecy!   The restoration and the happy state of Israel and Judah, when converted to Christ their King, are foretold; also, the miseries of the nations that persecuted them and The Saints before The Second Coming of Christ!   All men must honor the Son as they honor the Father and come into the service and worship of God by Him, there is no other way to The Father but by Him!   Our gracious Lord pardons the sins of the Believer, and breaks off the yoke of sin and Satan, that we may serve God without fear in righteousness and true holiness before Him in all the remainder of our days, as **The Redeemed** Subjects of Christ our King.

(D)   <u>**THE PROPHET EZEKIEL FORETOLD THE GREAT TRIBULATION**</u>

The prophet Ezekiel, spoke of a time (before the end of time) when a scattered Israel shall be gathered out of the nations of the world and brought back to their homeland and shall be made to Pass under the Rod, of The Great Tribulation!   You should know that God performed this very prophecy by gathering the people of Israel and bringing them back into their homeland in **1948**.   Now they are being made to pass under the rod that Ezekiel spoke of during The Great Tribulation that will enable God to restore them and place the **Son of David** on the throne in Israel.   The Lord Jesus Christ, who shall put down all enemies of Israel and God, will rule over Israel and the world for 1000 years before restoring all rulership back to God!

> *(Ezekiel 20:34-38) And I will bring you out from the people, and will gather you out of the countries wherein ye are scattered, with a mighty hand, and with a stretched out arm, and with fury poured out. And I will bring you into The Wilderness of the People, and there will I plead with you face to face. Like as I pleaded with your fathers in the wilderness of the land of Egypt, so will I plead with you, saith the Lord GOD. And I will cause you to pass under the rod, and I will bring you into the bond of the covenant:*

Now let's expound on the terms **The Wilderness of the People, and** Pass Under the Rod! The Wilderness of the People, figuratively speaking, a wilderness consisting of exile and oppression among foreigners, in which the wheat shall be sifted from the chaff.   In restoring His people from captivity, God will repeat to them the discipline to which He subjected their fathers, under Moses, in the literal wilderness of the Sinai, and by which He destroyed the rebellious from among them. To Pass Under the Rod as shepherds do their flocks, is symbolic to the numbering and reviewing each sheep of the fold, and separating the evil from the good. God has never forgotten the promises He made to Abraham, Isaac and Jacob regarding Israel and all His promises shall be fulfilled when He delivers them from The Great Tribulation and places Jesus Christ upon the Throne of David.

Also, notice in The Book of Ezekiel that God is going to cast Israel, during The Great Tribulation, into His Melting Pot, where they are to be refined as gold is refined. Israel, compared with other nations, had been as the gold and silver compared with baser metals. But they are now as the waste that is consumed in the furnace or thrown away when the silver is refined. Sinners, especially backsliding professors, are, in God's account, useless and fit for nothing. When God brings His own people into the furnace, during The Great Tribulation, He sits by them as the refiner by His gold, to see that they are not continued there any longer than is fitting and needful.   The dross shall be wholly separated, and the good metal purified.

> *(Ezekiel 22: 19-22) Therefore thus saith the Lord GOD; Because ye*

are all become dross, behold, therefore I will gather you into the midst of Jerusalem. As they gather silver, and brass, and iron, and lead, and tin, into the midst of the furnace, to blow the fire upon it, to melt it; so will I gather you in mine anger and in my fury, and I will leave you there, and melt you. Yea, I will gather you, and blow upon you in the fire of my wrath, and ye shall be melted in the midst thereof. As silver is melted in the midst of the furnace, so shall ye be melted in the midst thereof; and ye shall know that I the LORD have poured out my fury upon you.

This is the way of the Lord to test and try all of His people, refining them for entrance into the higher realms of glory!   In the test and trials of life, you seem to have failed the test, and thus, were left behind, **but God has sent me to tell you that He still loves you and cares about you!** Those of you who suffered pain in your life, or lingering sickness, and found that your hearts could scarcely bear even light and momentary afflictions, **God has not forgotten you!**   Although you were warned to flee from the wrath to come, and although you may have been deceived by the enemy and refused to obey, **God is seeking you out now!**   I just ask you to now seek and stand in truth for now you are facing the greatest trial of your life, **but God has promised to see you through if you trust Him**!   **Let this final trial you must face be sanctified by the power of the Holy Spirit, to the cleansing of your heart and hands from sin, that the far worse thing of eternal separation and damnation shall not come upon your soul!**

CHAPTER 4
SAINTS BELIEVED IN RESURRECTION

WHAT THIS CHAPTER IS ABOUT
IN CHAPTER 3 IT WAS ILLUSTRATED THAT JESUS AND THE PROPHETS SPOKE OF
THE FACT THAT GREAT TRIBULATION WAS COMING UPON THE EARTH! IN THIS
CHAPTER, I WISH TO REINFORCE THE REALITY THAT THE RESURRECTION OF
THE DEAD WAS SOMETHING THE SAINTS KNEW GOD WAS CAPABLE OF! AND YES,
THE RAPTURE HAS ACTUALLY TAKEN PLACE! THERE IS ONE RESURRECTION
LEFT AND YOU MUST BE A PART OF IT OR YOU WILL BE LOST FOR ETERNITY!
AGAIN, THE RESURECTION OF THE DEAD IS KNOWN AND BELEIVED BY ALL THE
CHILDREN OF GOD!

What I am about to teach you is vital to your understanding
of what is actually happening in the Plan of God!   It was God's
intention from the beginning to save all of mankind that conforms
to His will and to make salvation possible through Jesus Christ!
God knew that the fallen angel Lucifer (Satan) was present and
knew that Adam and Eve would be tempted along with all of
mankind!   But God used the temptation of man to try him to see
if he was worthy to walk with God! After Adam fell, God in His
foreknowledge already had The Plan of Salvation that would
deliver mankind from damnation! The Plan of Salvation must be
received and accepted by each soul that travels through the earth
realm! Since by man came death into humanity when Adam
disobeyed God and brought sin into the world, it would take a man
to deliver him or pay the price for his sins. Man, the first man,
sinned, and death came upon his race, because in him the race had
sinned. In Adam (in his seed) all die; all having become sinners
through him, as stated in **(See Romans 5:12,17-19).**   In Christ
shall all be made alive; He shall raise to life the whole human family
(See John 5:28-29); these scripture shows that Christ will raise
from the dead both the righteous and the wicked of all humanity,
because He has the power over Death and Hell!

Currently, I feel it is imperative that I give you some biblical background regarding the teaching of the scriptures concerning the reality of RESURRECTION! It seems all the Biblical greats knew without a doubt that God has resurrection power, that the dead could be raised!   I want you to grasp this because it will allow you to understand our main topic, focus and study of this entire book centers on, **THE FIRST RESURRECTION!** In Chapter (11) I shall go in-depth regarding how Jesus is utilizing THE FIRST RESURRECTION to gather all the righteous from the planet, both those who have died, and those who were alive when He came in the air!   I need you to understand that **resurrection** is real and God is real with all power, but now let's study what the scriptures reveals about this phenomenon!

(A) <u>WHY WOULD ABRAHAM SACRIFICE HIS SON?</u>

<u>(Genesis 22:5)</u> And Abraham said unto his young men, Abide ye here with the ass; and I and the lad will go yonder and worship, and come again to you.

Abraham knew he was taking his only son to sacrifice him to God, but he made the statement to his servants, I and the lad will-- come again; he believed that though he offered his son as a sacrifice in obedience to God, God could raise Isaac from the dead, or in some way restore him, so he affirmed his conviction! **(See Hebrews 11:17-19).**   Even when Isaac asked him**, *my father: and he said, here am I, my son. And he said, Behold the fire and the wood: but where is the lamb for a burnt offering? And Abraham said, my son, God will provide himself a lamb for a burnt offering: so, they went both together.*** What powerful faith in God, a permanent conviction that God will provide, is a sure and steadfast anchor to the soul. Under its influence, though the winds rage and the tempests roar, men may outride the storm, and in due time calmly and joyfully enter the port. That is the stance of a true Christian or Saint, to believe heartily and fully the divine declarations, and expect their fulfilment; it is not necessary to know, or be able to conceive, how they can be accomplished. Abraham just believed God, that is why

God called him **The Father of Faith!**

<u>God is asking you in this dark hour to just believe in Him and He will safely bring you through the storm, to a shore of peace and everlasting joy, to a place filled with His glory!</u>

(B) <u>THE BOOK OF HEBREWS SAYS ABOUT THE FAITH OF ABRAHAM</u>

<u>(Hebrews 11:19)</u> Accounting that God was able to raise him up, even from the dead; from whence also he received him in a figure.

It tells us in the book of Hebrews **(Hebrews 11:17, 18)** that Abraham knew the promise of God to him, that his only son Isaac was to be the expansion of His seed and the expansion of God's people, therefore he knew that though he offered him, God would restore him!   In a figure, Abraham believed Isaac would raise alive from the altar where he expected him to die. There are no difficulties in believing God's declarations and obeying His commands, because faith brings victory.

We are often called to leave worldly connections, interests, and comforts. If heirs of Abraham's faith, we shall obey and go forth, though not knowing what may befall us; and we shall be found in the way of duty, looking for the performance of God's promises. The trial of Abraham's faith was, that he simply and fully obeyed the call of God. Many, who have a part in the promises, do not soon receive the things promised. Faith can lay hold of blessings at a great distance; can make them present; can love them and rejoice in them, though strangers; as saints, whose home is Heaven; as pilgrims, travelling toward their home. By faith, they overcome the terrors of death, and bid a cheerful farewell to this world, and to all the comforts and crosses of it. And those who are once truly saved are called out of a sinful state, have no mind to return into it. All true Believers desire the Heavenly inheritance; and the stronger faith is, the more fervent those desires will be.

Notwithstanding their meanness by nature, their vileness by sin, and the poverty of their outward condition, God is not ashamed to be called the God of all true believers; such is His mercy, such is His love to them. Let them never be ashamed of being called His people, nor of any of those who are truly so, how much so ever despised in the world. Above all, let them take care that they are not a shame and reproach to their God. The greatest trial and act of faith upon record is, Abraham's offering up Isaac, **(Genesis 22:2).** There, every word shows a trial. It is our duty to reason down our doubts and fears, by looking, as Abraham did, to the Almighty power of God. The best way to enjoy our comforts is, to give them up to God; He will then again give them as shall be the best for us. Let us look how far our faith has caused the like obedience, when we have been called to lesser acts of self-denial, or to make smaller sacrifices to our duty. Have we given up what was called for, fully believing that the Lord would make up all our losses, and even bless us through the most afflicting experiences?

(C) <u>JOB TESTIFIES THAT JESUS WILL RETURN IN THE END OF TIME</u>

> ***(<u>Job 19:25-27</u>) For I know that my Redeemer liveth, and that He shall stand at the latter day upon the earth: And though after my skin worms destroy this body, yet in my flesh shall I see God: Whom I shall see for myself, and mine eyes shall behold, and not another; though my reins be consumed within me.***

These verses render a strong confidence in an Almighty, Ever-Living Redeemer, and the expectation of meeting Him as a friend and portion, support the soul in the deepest affliction, causing it to rejoice in the Hope of the Glory of God. Job in his suffering says; After my skin; or after his body shall have been destroyed by disease and worms consume his body in physical death, he affirms that in his flesh; the literal rendering is, from my flesh, he shall still stand before God. This is taken by some to mean, looking forth upon God from my body of flesh, that is, <u>after its resurrection</u>, which is the idea given here, yet in my flesh shall I see God!   I love the words of Job as he ends this passage by saying "Though my reins be consumed within me;" which I interpret him meaning though his mind may consume, he still shall see God for himself! Job knew that we all shall resurrect and stand before God!

(D) <u>PROPHET ISAIAH PROPHECIES OF THE DEAD RISING</u>

(Isaiah 26:19) Thy dead men shall live, together with my dead body shall they arise. Awake and sing, ye that dwell in dust: for thy dew is as the dew of herbs, and the earth shall cast out the dead.

The dead; the dead of God's people. The life-giving power of God is now set in strong contrast with the weakness of man. Together with my dead body shall I arise; or, our dead bodies shall arise. Thy dew; the dew, that is, the quickening power that descends upon God's people, is as the dew of herbs; has, like the dew falling on herbs, a life-giving power.   Some understand this verse speaks of a Spiritual Resurrection, **(See Ezekiel 37:1-14);** others, of the resurrection of the body, and this seems to have been the interpretation of the ancient Jews. As Christ triumphed over death and hell in His own resurrection, and will at **The Last Day** make all His people triumphant over both, He must be able to grant them all needed help and deliverance in their present conflict with the powers of darkness. This meaning Jesus will help you if you trust Him to stand on His Word!   All have sinned and come short of the Glory of God at some stage in their lives, all have been slaves of sin and Satan; but by the Divine grace we can look to be set free from all former masters. The cause opposed to God and His Kingdom is about to sink at last. May your afflictions be presented to Jesus through prayer! May your petitions to Him come drop by drop; may now you pour it out, may they come forth now like water from a fountain!   Praise God, afflictions bring us to secret prayer! Consider what Christ has done for those who believe, His resurrection from the dead: our own deliverance as foretold by the Bible! The power of His grace, like the dew or rain, which causes the herbs that seem dead to revive, would raise His Church from the lowest state. But we may refer to The Resurrection of the Dead, especially those united to Christ, to be the crown act of deliverance!

(E) <u>THE PROPHET DANIEL REVEALS THE DEAD WILL AWAKEN IN THE LAST DAYS</u>

(Daniel 12:2,13) And many of them that sleep in the dust of the earth shall awake, some to everlasting life, and some to shame and everlasting contempt. But go thou thy way till the end be: for thou shalt rest, and stand in thy lot at the end of the days.

Daniel says **<u>Many of them that sleep</u>;** probably the same as the multitude of them that sleep or have died: **(Compare Romans 5:19).** This passage of scripture is when the Angel of the Lord passes immediately from the last great struggle with Antichrist (The Great Tribulation) to the final resurrection and judgment. The final resurrection and judgment will complete, on the one hand, the triumph of Christ and His church, and on the other, the destruction of Satan and his followers!

<u>Go thou thy way till the end</u>; the Angel dismisses Daniel with an indication that he must wait till the time of the end for a clear understanding of the vision. **<u>For thou shalt rest</u>;** with God, after his departure from this life, though Daniel's body shall be in the grave, his spirit shall be resting with the Lord! The Angel reveals that Daniel shall have his part in his lot, in the possession of his Heavenly inheritance. **(Compare Daniel 12:3).**

<u>At the end of the days</u>, at the time referred to in **(Daniel 12:2)** is a reference to this, **The End of Time!** It is of comparatively little importance in what part of the world's history our life occurs, since, when the glorious end comes, all who are in Christ shall be present to rejoice in it with joy unspeakable and full of glory. All opposing the rule of Christ: all principality, and power, shall be put down, and holiness and love will triumph! The end of the rule of evil shall come. What an amazing prophecy is this, of so many varied events, and extending through so many successive ages, even to the general resurrection!   Daniel must comfort himself with the pleasing prospect of his own happiness in death, and in judgment, that will lead to a joyfulness in eternity! It is necessary for you to think much of going away from this world!   The true Church has been Raptured, now what must you do next?   Devotion to Christ must be your way; but it is your belief that you will not leave this world till God calls you to another world, for He holds your life in His hands! Until He says, go thou thy way, thou hast done thy work, therefore now, go thy way, and leave it to others who shall come after you!

> **(_Revelation 6:10-11_) And they cried with a loud voice, saying, how long, O Lord, Holy and True, dost Thou not judge and avenge our blood on them that dwell on the earth? And white robes were given unto every one of them; and it was said unto them, that they should rest yet for a little season, until their fellow servants also and their brethren, that should be killed as they were, should be fulfilled.**

It was a comfort to Daniel, and is a comfort to all the Saints, that whatever their predicament is in the days of their lives, they shall have a happy result in the **End of Days!**   And it ought to be with great care and concern of every one of us, to secure this knowledge. In giving some words of comfort to you, my Brother or Sister: Though you have been Left Behind, still be thankful that you are gaining the understanding that even in your present state (being in the Great Tribulation), you still have a chance to be welcomed into Glory; it is the will of God!   May you rest your faith in God now, that your faith may strengthen you to reserve your place in Heaven!

(F)   <u>ELISHA RAISES A CHILD FROM THE DEAD</u>

> **(_2King 4:32-35_) And when Elisha was come into the house, behold, the child was dead, and laid upon his bed. He went in therefore, and shut the door upon them twain, and prayed unto the LORD. And he went up, and lay upon the child, and put his mouth upon his mouth, and his eyes upon his eyes, and his hands upon his hands:**

and he stretched himself upon the child; and the flesh of the child waxed warm. Then he returned, and walked in the house to and fro; and went up, and stretched himself upon him: and the child sneezed seven times, and the child opened his eyes.

The Prophet Elisha had a strong belief in the power of God to raise one from the dead!

(G) <u>A DEAD MAN COMES TO LIFE AFTER HAVING TOUCHED THE BONES OF ELISHA</u>

(<u>2 King 13:21</u>) And it came to pass, as they were burying a man, that, behold, they spied a band of men; and they cast the man into the sepulchre of Elisha: and when the man was let down, and touched the bones of Elisha, he revived, and stood up on his feet.

Elisha had died and his body was buried in a sunken tomb. The Moabites had invaded the land and a band of Moabites were spying out some men in the land who were in the process of burying a man that was dead!   These men doing the burying knew that they were near the tomb of the Great Prophet Elisha and knowing the exploits of the deceased prophet when living, they decided to lower the dead man's body into Elisha's tomb to touch Elisha's bones!   Guess what, the dead man was revived, resurrected and stood up on his feet! The spies watching this were astonished! This is showing that God was with the Great Prophet Elisha after his death, as much as before!   The presence of God with His people is not confined to this life; He answers to their prayers while here, He will still, after they are dead, bestow great blessings and power upon His people!

(H) <u>JESUS CHRIST ILLUSTRATES RESURRECTION POWER</u>

The supernatural power of God to raise the dead was illustrated in the words and works of Jesus Christ, let us look at some examples:

(1)

<u>JESUS RAISES THE MAID FROM THE DEAD</u>

(<u>Matthew 9:24-25</u>)   He said unto them, Give place: for the maid is not dead, but sleepeth. And they laughed him to scorn. But when the people were put forth, he went in, and took her by the hand, and the maid arose.

Give place or simply said, move out of the way, or get out, your services are not wanted. She is not dead; that is, not permanently. Her death or the death of her body is but as a sleep from which she will be speedily awakened!   The reality of the death is not denied, but please understand that death only affects the physical body not your spirit; it is eternal!   The fact utterly assumed by those that believe is that death will be followed by a resurrection, as sleep is by an awakening. Because Jesus said the maid was sleep, the unbelievers laughed Him to scorn!   The company of mourners was certain that the child was dead and, understanding neither the language nor the power of Jesus, laughed in derision!   Jesus went in; Mark tells us that He took with him five persons. When the people were put out. Luke says that Peter, James and John, and the father and mother of the maiden were permitted to remain **(Luke 8:51**). He took her by the hand. As we learn from one of the parallel accounts, He said to her, Talitha cumi **(Mark 5:41) this** is Aramaic, the language generally spoken by the common people in Palestine at the time of Christ. The words mean: Rise, my child! They were immediately obeyed. She arose and walked. **(Mark 5:37-40).** These were all competent witnesses, as were the multitude when they saw her walk out, of the reality of the miracle.

(2)
<u>JESUS RAISES THE ONLY SON OF A WIDOW FROM THE DEAD</u>

(<u>Luke 7:12-15</u>) Now when he came nigh to the gate of the city, behold, there was a dead man carried out, the only son of his mother, and she was a widow: and much people of the city was with her. And when the Lord saw her, he had compassion on her, and said unto her, Weep not. And he came and touched the bier: and

they that bare him stood still. And he said, Young man, I say unto thee, Arise. And he that was dead sat up and began to speak. And he delivered him to his mother.

No sorrows of a Christian mother, especially a widowed mother on the death of an only son, escape the tender and sympathizing notice of the Savior. His bosom swells with pity; and when she thinks not of it, He is preparing to pour into her wounded spirit the balm of consolation and cause the desolate, sorrowing heart to sing for joy! Came nigh to the gate. Like most Oriental towns it had walls and a gate. Just outside of the gate He met the funeral procession. The dead were always carried out of a Jewish city for burial. Jesus saw a dead man carried out on a bier, the body covered by a cloth, but not in a coffin.   The only son of his mother! Such a loss to a Jewish widow would be too great for consolation **(See Jeremiah 6:26; Amos 8:10; Zechariah 12:10).** Jesus had compassion, for sorrow or need always touches His loving heart.   Jesus told the mother, Weep not! How often has Jesus has dried up the fountains of sorrow?   Jesus then touched the bier as a signal to stop. There was authority in not only the words but the acts of the Lord which compelled obedience! Then Jesus spoke one Word to the dead son which was - Arise**!**   This is the first time He spoke these words to the dead, the first time He revealed He was **THE RESURRECTION AND LIFE**!   It must have been to His disciples and the multitude a moment of suspense and wonder. The child sat up. As the daughter of Jairus **(Mark 5:41-42),** and Lazarus **(John 11:43-44),** so the widow's son at once obeyed, arose and spoke! The Lord finished His work by taking him by the hand and presenting him to his mother. Language could not express her joy!   One Word from Jesus and the dead rose and shall rise!

(3)
<u>JESUS RAISES LAZARUS FROM THE DEAD</u>

<u>(John 11:43-44)</u>   And when he thus had spoken, he cried with a loud voice, Lazarus, come forth. And he that was dead came forth, bound hand and foot with graveclothes: and his face was bound about with

a napkin. Jesus saith unto them, loose him, and let him go.

Jesus had already proven that He had resurrection power but at the grave of Lazarus, He cried with a loud voice. It is suggested that the voice was like the sound of many waters **(Revelation 1:15),** at which all who are in their graves shall come forth **(1Thessalonians 4:16).** It was the voice of authority. And he that was dead came forth! The earth had never beheld a more wonderful or startling sight. At once the sleeping body of Lazarus arose and came forth, bound with his grave clothes, with the napkin still upon his face that had been bound under his jaw to keep it from falling. The lookers-on, astonished and dazed, were only recalled to themselves when the Lord bade them, loose him and let him go. He spoke as the Divine Word, and death obeyed. As He cried to Lazarus, come forth **(John 11:43),** so shall He speak with the voice of an archangel to all that are in their graves, and they shall come forth and live **(1Thessalonians 4:16).** <u>**Can you trust Him**</u>?

(4)
<u>JESUS SPEAKS OF HIS OWN RESURRECTION FROM THE DEAD</u>

<u>(John 10:18)</u> No man taketh it from me, but I lay it down of myself. I have power to lay it down, and I have power to take it again. This commandment have I received of my Father.

Jesus set the record straight that He has power over life and death, can you believe this? The God of all creation stated, <u>**no man taketh my life**</u> for no man had power to take His life till He should voluntarily surrender Himself to crucifixion and death. <u>**This commandment have I received**</u>; He was commissioned of God to die for the sins of men, and rise again for their justification, and He obeyed The Father! He had the power, disposition, and right to do these things. <u>**I lay it down of myself.**</u> His life. He gave Himself for man of His free will. He laid it down on the cross; He took it up when He rose from the dead. **(Read the lesson in**

John 10:1-18):   The Lord Jesus knows those who are His, whom he has chosen, and is sure of them; they also know whom they have trusted and are sure of Him. I see here the grace of Christ; since none could demand His life of Him, He laid it down of Himself for our redemption. He offered Himself to be our Savior! And the necessity of our case calling for it, He offered Himself for the Sacrifice.   He was both the offeror and the offering, so that His laying down His life was His offering up Himself.   It is plain, He was our substitute, that He died in our place; to obtain that we may be set free from the punishment of sin, to obtain the pardon for our sin; and that only His death could obtain that pardon. Our Lord laid not His life down for His doctrine, but for His sheep. Can you accept and believe this, if so, ask Him to be your Shepherd!

(5)

JESUS ROSE FROM THE DEAD HIMSELF, THE TOMB WAS EMPTY

(Luke 24:2-8) And they found the stone rolled away from the sepulchre. And they entered in and found not the body of the Lord Jesus. And it came to pass, as they were much perplexed thereabout, behold, two men stood by them in shining garments: And as they were afraid, and bowed down their faces to the earth, they said unto them, Why seek ye the living among the dead? He is not here, but is risen: remember how He spake unto you when He was yet in Galilee, Saying, The Son of man must be delivered into the hands of sinful men, and be crucified, and the third day rise again. And they remembered His words,

The resurrection of Christ **(Luke 24:1-12)**.   Jesus appears to two disciples on the way to Emmaus **(Luke 24:13-27)** and makes Himself known to them **(Luke 24:28-35)**. Christ appears to the other disciples **(Luke 24:36-49)** after His ascension **(Luke 24:50-53)**

(6)

AFTER THE RESURRECTION OF JESUS THE GRAVES WERE OPENED

(Matthew 27:52-53) And the graves were opened; and many bodies of the saints which slept arose, And came out of the graves after is resurrection, and went into the holy city, and appeared unto many.

The tombs were opened. The convulsions of the earth would naturally roll the stones from the doors of the sepulchers. The Bible explicitly states the many bodies of The Saints that slept arose! The spirits of the Saints were confined in the prison house of Hell in the paradise section before Christ arrived and conquered death and Hell, taking their keys or power! Those Saints which slept; were Saints who were physically dead, but they arose. Their bodies arose once Jesus set free their spirits; they arose by reentering their bodies and rising! I will cover more of this in **Chapter 11 on PHASE 1 OF THE FIRST RESURRECTION!** So, what we see here is that after his resurrection in trigger a resurrection of The Saints who had died before His resurrection, they were raised. Their rising was a testimony that the death of Christ is life to the Saints. The whole transaction was designed to show that through the resurrection of Christ, His disciples shall also attain to a glorious resurrection.

(I) <u>PETER AND PAUL ILLUSTRATE RESURRECTION POWER</u>

(1)
<u>THE APOSTLES PETER AND PAUL RAISE INDIVIDUALS FROM THE DEAD</u>

(Acts 9:36-41) Now there was at Joppa a certain disciple named Tabitha, which by interpretation is called Dorcas: this woman was full of good works and alms deeds which she did. And it came to pass in those days, that she was sick, and died: whom when they had washed, they laid her in an upper chamber. And forasmuch as Lydda was nigh to Joppa, and the disciples had heard that Peter was there, they sent unto him two men, desiring him that he would not delay coming to them. Then Peter arose and went with them. When he was come, they brought him into the upper chamber: and all the widows stood by him weeping, and shewing the coats and garments which Dorcas made, while she was with them. But Peter put them all forth, and kneeled, and prayed; and turning him to the

body said, Tabitha, arise. And she opened her eyes: and when she saw Peter, she sat up. And he gave her his hand, and lifted her up, and when he had called the saints and widows, presented her alive.

Here The Apostle Peter was summoned to the home of Tabitha, or Dorcas in the Greek (meaning gazelle), a saintly Christian noted for her deeds of love who had died. She had been washed, meaning her body had been prepared for burial and was lying in wait in her upper chamber. The place was the large upper room on the upper floor of Eastern houses, usually used as a guest chamber. The Saints in Joppa sent two men for the Apostle Peter because the fame of his miracles was so well known that they probably hoped that he might restore her to life. When Peter came the widows stood by him weeping. They had been the objects of her benevolence. Persons who are very benevolent and useful in life, will be affectionately remembered, and greatly lamented in death; and all their works performed from love to God and to men, will meet a gracious and abundant reward. Peter put them all forth, or removed them, out of the chamber for the time was not to weep but to trust God **(Compare 1Kings 17:19-23; 2Kings 4:32-36; Matthew 9:25).** When praying and believing God, one must fix your whole soul on the Lord in prayer. Peter knelt on his knees to the Lord trusting in His power! In his prayer he called on the name of Christ, was answered, and only needed to say, 'Tabitha, arise', and she opened her eyes. There is power in the name of Jesus! It was the first miracle in which death was overcome at the hands of an Apostle. Many believed in the Lord; the Lord Jesus, whom Peter preached, and by whose power he wrought this great miracle.

(2)

APOSTLE PAUL RAISES EUTYCHUS FROM THE DEAD

(Acts 20:9-10) And there sat in a window a certain young man named Eutychus, being fallen into a deep sleep: and as Paul was long preaching, he sunk down with sleep, and fell down from the third loft, and was taken up dead. And Paul went down, and fell on him, and embracing him said, Trouble not yourselves; for his life is

in him.

The Bible illustrates the account of Eutychus, a Saint who was sitting in the window of an upper chamber during a Church Meeting where the Apostle Paul was preaching!   It seems Paul was a long-winded speaker and Eutychus, overcome by drowsiness, fell three stories to the ground below. The language implies that he was killed by the fall, and resurrected by the Divine power of Jesus Christ, exercised through Paul!

CHAPTER 5
YOU MUST BE BORN-AGAIN, THIS IS HOW!

WHAT THIS CHAPTER IS ABOUT
IN CHAPTER 4 I DISCUSSED THE RESURRECTION POWER OF JESUS CHRIST IS REAL! IN THIS CHAPTER THE DRIVING FAITH OF ALL BELIEVERS IN CHRIST IS THAT THEY CAN LIVE FOREVER WITH GOD IN GLORY!   HAVING DISCUSSED RESURRECTION AND THE SURETY OF IT, THE SAINTS KNOW THAT ETERNAL LIFE IS NOT HINDERED BY DEATH.   BUT, NO ONE CAN ENTER INTO GOD'S KINGDOM EXCEPT SUCH A ONE ACCEPTS GOD'S SON, JESUS CHRIST, AND THAT ACCEPTANCE MUST BE IMPLEMENTED AS A SPIRITUAL REBIRTH! I WANT NOW TO DISCUSS WITH YOU, AS WE CONTINUE OUR STUDY ON YOU BEING LEFT BEHIND, HOW TRUE SALVATION IS OBTAINED AND THE FACT, THOUGH LEFT BEHIND, YOU CAN STILL RECEIVE IT!

Being a Christian is not an intellectual reality, for God, who is a Spirit, cannot be known through your flesh (you can't mentally or physically actually know God or make yourself into a Christian). As said in, *(John 4:24)*, *God is a Spirit: and they that worship Him must worship Him in spirit and in truth.* Today, many know OF GOD with their minds, but do not truly KNOW GOD with their spirits! Knowing God means to have a heart to please Him, which is pleasing to God!   Having a spirit to keep the commandments of God will be the result of those that love Him. For obedience is the fruit of love.

> *(John 14:15) says, if ye love Me, keep my commandments.*
> *(John 3:3,5)   Jesus answered and said unto him, Verily, verily, I say unto thee, except a man be born again, he cannot see the Kingdom of God. Jesus answered, Verily, verily, I say unto thee, except a man be born of water and of the Spirit, he cannot enter the Kingdom of God.*

Please understand that The Kingdom of God is spiritual in nature, it is a **Spiritual Kingdom** and can only be entered by the spirit of man **(THE INNER MAN)!** When the inner man, which is <u>your spirit</u>, comes in union or allows the Holy Spirit of God to access your <u>inner most being</u> or sanctuary, then and only then will you become open or accessible to The Kingdom of God! **It is within you;** the true reign of Christ is in the hearts of men! A Kingdom that has its throne in the heart, (meaning rulership over your spirit), on which Christ, the King, sits!   It must be formed by yielding your heart or submitting your spirit to Christ!   I know that many of you may not understand what I am saying at this time, Nicodemus did not understand it either! But what I am trying to get you to see before I even continue is that: The Kingdom of God is an inner-kingdom, not an outer-kingdom! You discover it on the inside of your innermost being, it cannot be accessed by outside works of the flesh! I pray you can understand what I am saying here! Take a look at these scriptures:

> ***(Luke 17:20,21)*** *And when He was demanded of the Pharisees, when The Kingdom of God should come, He answered them and said, The Kingdom of God cometh not with observation: Neither shall they say, Lo here! or, lo there! For, behold, the Kingdom of God is within you.*

Jesus reveals that without **THE REBIRTH,** one cannot see (comprehend) or **ENTER INTO** (access) The Kingdom of God! Cannot **see** meaning one cannot comprehend the reality of **The Kingdom of God** or the reality that the spiritual world truly exists! And one cannot **enter** meaning: without being **Born-Again** one cannot go-to, be a citizen of, or enter its gates unless one is Born-Again!

> ***(John 3:6)*** *That which is born of the flesh is flesh; and that which is born of the Spirit is spirit.*

<u>**Born of the flesh**</u> is flesh —means by the natural birth, fleshly children come from fleshly parents; <u>**Born of the Spirit**</u> is spirit - by the spiritual re-birth, spiritual children come from the Holy Spirit! Flesh and spirit are opposed to each other. The first denotes what is earthly and impure; the second, what is Heavenly and Holy. THE REBIRTH is the life and power of Jesus Christ **operating**

within which causes one to pursue right relationship with God based on faith!   I like the term rebirth because spiritually it means that your spirit has been reborn or re-opened to God and His Kingdom, The Kingdom of God! You know that Adam's spirit was shut off from God because of sin, and all of humanity was shut off from God because of Adam, but the REBIRTH opens one back up to have access to God and His Kingdom!   The enemy, Satan, has erroneously converted the worship of God to an **OUTWARD RITUAL,** when in reality; a true relationship with God is an **INNER REALITY,** which is revealed outwardly!

TO TRULY BE BORN-AGAIN ONE MUST MAKE A SPIRITUAL TRANSACTION WITH GOD!

(<u>Romans 10:9,10</u>) That if thou shalt confess with thy mouth the Lord Jesus, and shalt believe in thine heart that God hath raised Him from the dead, thou shalt be saved.' For with the heart man believeth unto righteousness; and with the mouth confession is made unto salvation.

<u>Confess with thy mouth</u>--<u>believe in thy heart</u>; the Apostle Paul mentions these two things, because both are necessary for true salvation—you are to have an inward faith in Christ, and the outward confession of Him. That He is the Son of God that personally died for your sins and God has raised Him from the dead!   By raising Christ from the dead, God set His seal to Him as the promised Messiah. Because if thou shalt confess with thy mouth Jesus as Lord!   Notice the importance which Jesus attached to confession, for with confession is tied the fact that you know you were a hopeless sinner, and understand the wrath of God that is tied to sin and that Jesus has delivered you from your hopeless condition, if you accept Him in your heart as Savior!

Jesus says in *(<u>Matthew 10:32</u>) Whosoever therefore shall confess me before men, him will I confess also before my Father which is in Heaven* and
(<u>Luke 12:8</u>) Also I say unto you, Whosoever shall confess Me before men, him shall the Son of man also confess before the Angels of

God; and compare
(<u>Acts 8:37</u>) And Philip said, If thou believes with all thine heart, thou mayest. And he answered and said, I believe that Jesus Christ is the Son of God.

To openly confess Christ, not be ashamed of Him, even in days of persecution is a trial of faith of the severest kind. Note distinctly that there is no promise here to a concealed faith; those who are ashamed of Jesus before an evil and sinful world.   And **<u>shalt believe in thine heart</u>**. That is, with all the heart, **in the inner man, in the spirit of man**. The belief must not be only a mental approval, but a belief that brings the whole man or woman to **<u>repentance</u>**, a desire to change one's life and lifestyle to follow Christ, that extends into loving trust and obedience to Christ!

<u>Thou shalt be saved</u>. The promise of Christ made plain! Such a faith confessed unites its subject to Christ as His loving subject, and imparts to him the righteousness of those who have died to sin and been freed from the law.

(<u>Romans 6:1-4</u>) says, What shall we say then? Shall we continue in sin, that grace may abound? God forbids. How shall we, that are dead to sin, live any longer therein? Know ye not, that so many of us as were baptized into Jesus Christ were baptized into His death? Therefore we are buried with Him by baptism into death: that like as Christ was raised up from the dead by the glory of the Father, even so we also should walk in newness of life..

So how are you to truly come into the Body of Christ, The Christian Church, The Family of the Living God? **ONLY,** I say **ONLY, BY THE REBIRTH**, and that rebirth is forged with God by you making a personal spiritual transaction with God, **<u>coming to Him personally,</u>** not through another! **<u>Acknowledging you are a sinner and repenting of your sins;</u>** asking Jesus, who is standing there wherever you are, to come into your heart as your Savior!! That transaction must be from the heart! Now look within, focus your spirit inward, turn to Jesus now, acknowledging that His death on the cross, and His burial, and resurrection from the dead was for your personal forgiveness of sin! Ask Jesus to come into your heart, your inner man, your spirit and believe He is entering the inside of you!   Now with all your strength receive Him and begin to vocally **THANK HIM, THANK HIM, THANK HIM FOR SAVING YOU!!!** Now my Brother or Sister, just **TURN FROM SIN AND SUBMIT YOURSELF TO FOLLOWING THE LORD JESUS CHRIST!**   If that transaction is true, the Holy Spirit will come into your heart (your spirit or inner man) and spiritually baptize (or place you) into **The Body of Christ, The Church!** You have just made a spiritual transaction with God to accept **Jesus Christ!!!!** The Holy Spirit will come and abide in you and you will, spiritually abide in Christ and He will open you up to **The Spirit of God** and to **(The Kingdom of God)!**   You spiritually become a part of Christ and Christ becomes a part of you! When that transaction occurs, you become a new creature, old things are passed away and you become new!   You will no longer love the world nor the things of the world, you will come out of darkness and be translated into The Light! You are now changed, a new creation, you are not the same! You are born-again, you are now in **The Family of God**!

My Brother or Sister, as I communicate with you I want you to know if you had never made such a deep felt personal communication and transaction with God, it means you have never been truly Born-Again!   To clarify further, it means you had never truly been spiritually converted!   The rebirth must occur in your spirit not in your mind and many have missed the mark in this area of receiving the Lord Jesus and becoming a true Christian! If you have had trouble serving God and being faithful to Him, it could be you were never truly Born-Again!   If this **spiritual transaction** did not take place in your past, **YOU WERE NOT TRULY HIS** (Christ) and were never in the true **Christian Church! Congratulations Saint of the Most High God!**

CHAPTER 6
WHAT DID JESUS SAY ABOUT THE RAPTURE?
WHAT THIS CHAPTER IS ABOUT

IN CHAPTER 5 I DISCUSSED THE REBIRTH OR HOW TO BE BORN-AGAIN! NOW I
WISH TO INTENSLY EXAMINE WHAT THE RAPTURE IS! THE RAPTURE OF THE
CHRISTIAN CHURCH HAS OCCURRED AND ALL THOSE WHO WERE TRULY BORN-
AGAIN AND DEDICATED TO CHRIST HAVE BEEN TAKEN, BOTH THE LIVING AND
THE DEAD! JESUS, THE PROPHETS, AND THE APOSTLES PREDICTED THAT SUCH
AN EVENT WOULD OCCUR BEFORE THE SECOND COMING OF CHRIST! WELL, IT
HAS OCCURRED! NOW THAT YOU UNDERSTAND (1) WHAT TRUE SALVATION IS
AND SOME OF THE MISCONCEPTIONS YOU MAY HAVE HAD ABOUT THE TERM,
AND (2) RESURRECTION AND THAT IT WAS BELIEVED BY SAINTS OF ALL THE
AGES. LETS NOW GO INTO A DEEPER SPIRITUAL STUDY ABOUT THE RAPTURE, A
COMPONENT OF RESURRECTION. LET US LOOK INTO WHAT JESUS HIMSELF
HAD TO SAY ABOUT THE EVENT THAT HAS ALREADY TRANSPIRED!

The Rapture of the Church, which has taken place, is a primary
part of God's Plan to eternally deliver the righteous out of the
Earth prior to judging Satan, the forces of evil, the demon spirits
and wicked men and women! Jesus Himself went through great
lengths to teach many lessons and give extensive warnings that this
event would take place! I now want to expose you to the teachings
of Jesus Christ on this very important subject!!

(A) JESUS SPOKE THIS IN THE PARABLE OF THE WHEAT AND THE TARES

*(Matthew 13:24-27) Another parable put He forth unto them, saying,
The Kingdom of Heaven is likened unto a man which sowed good
seed in his field: But while men slept, his enemy came and sowed
tares among the wheat, and went his way. But when the blade was
sprung up, and brought forth fruit, then appeared the tares also. So,
the servants of the householder came and said unto him, Sir, didst
not thou sow good seed in thy field? from whence then hath it
tares? Let both grow together until the harvest: and in the time of
harvest I will say to the reapers, Gather ye together first the tares,
and bind them in bundles to burn them: but gather the wheat into
my barn.*

In this parable, The Harvest represents The End of Time and

The Day of Judgment. The Reapers are The Angels. The Tares represent The Wicked. The Wheat; represents the righteous. (Read the rest of **Matthew 13:49-50)**. Please understand that this parable represents the present and future state of the Gospel hearing church at the End of Time!   It shows Christ's care of it, the devil's enmity against it, and the mixture there is in it of good and bad members all confessing to be Christians! The parable also shows the separation between them in the other world or the next life (the spirit world). So prone is fallen man to sin, that if the enemy sow the tares, he may go his way, they will spring up, and do hurt; whereas, when good seed is sown, it must be tended, watered, and fenced. The servants complained to their master; Sir, didst thou not sow good seed in thy field? For you would think all those that profess Christ would be true! No doubt he did appeal to all; whatever is inappropriate in the church, I am sure it is not from Christ!   Though gross transgressors, and such as openly oppose the Gospel, ought to be separated from the society of the faithful, yet no human skill can make an exact separation. Those who oppose must not be cut off, but instructed, and that with meekness. And though good and bad are together in this world, yet at **The Great Day** they shall be parted; then the righteous and the wicked shall be plainly known; though sometimes it is hard to distinguish between them. Let us, knowing the terrors of the Lord, not do iniquity. At death, believers shall shine forth to themselves; and at The Great Day they shall shine forth before all the world. They shall shine by reflection, with light borrowed from the Fountain of light. Their sanctification will be made perfect, and their justification published. I pray, may we be found of that happy number.

(B) <u>JESUS STATES THAT NO ONE WILL KNOW WHEN THE RAPTURE WILL TAKE PLACE</u>

<u>(Mark 13:32</u>) But of that day and that hour knoweth no man, no, not the angels which are in heaven, neither the Son, but the Father.

Of that day when He would Rapture **The Church** or time when He would return knows no one, neither the Son!   When Jesus was on earth in the flesh, He voluntarily subjected Himself to limitations, among them ignorance of the hour when He would return to judgment. If He didn't know, how can or could anyone else know the day or hour? The day here spoken of was one of those things which the Son, as man, in the sense in which it is said: He increased in wisdom, did not know; as man: He neither knew, nor was commissioned to make it known. Nothing but the event itself of The Rapture revealed it!

(C)   JESUS FOREKNEW ALL WHO ARE TO BE SAVED FROM THE WRATH TO COME

(Luke 10:20) Notwithstanding in this rejoice not, that the spirits are subject unto you; but rather rejoice, because your names are written in Heaven.

Nothing shall by any means hurt you; the chief reference of these words is to the spiritual victory which Christ gives His servants over all evil, of which the outward deliverances sometimes granted to them in this world are symbols and pledges. **(Compare Romans 8:28, 37).** Christ can give His ministers all the aid which they need for the discharge of their duties. In His name and strength, they may commence their work, and go on from conquer to conquer, till every knee shall bow, and every tongue confess that He is Lord, to the glory of God the Father. Rejoice not in your own power as Judas had this power in Christ's name and failed to submit to its grace. But rather rejoice in the hope of salvation. The greatest of all subjects of rejoicing is that we are the Children of God, **and you can still be a Child of God if you just believe.**

(D)   JESUS SPOKE THE PARABLE OF ONE TAKEN AND ONE LEFT BEHIND

(Luke 17:34-37) I tell you, in that night there shall be two men in one bed; the one shall be taken, and the other shall be left. Two women shall be grinding together; the one shall be taken, and the

other left. Two men shall be in the field; the one shall be taken, and the other left. And they answered and said unto him, Where, Lord? And he said unto them, Wheresoever the body is, thither will the eagles be gathered together.

If I had to explain this parable to someone I would say: Faith in Christ is the great characteristic of a Saint, and the want of it, of a sinner. This makes a mighty difference in their character, condition, and prospects. Though they live in the same family, work in the same field, or sleep in the same bed, one, believing Christ, is led to follow His directions and be saved; the other, not believing Him, neglects His directions, and is lost! One shall be taken; the other shall be left behind **(Matthew 24:40-41.)** When, Lord? When will such calamities come? Wheresoever the body is; wherever the unbelievers are, there will their destroyers be upon them, as eagles upon their prey. **(Matthew 24:28.)** The Kingdom of God was among those professing to know Him, as well as within them that truly knew Him. It was a Spiritual Kingdom, set up in the heart by the power of Divine grace. Observe how it had been with sinners formerly, considering that they understood the judgments of God, which they had been warned of, yet, they continue to disobey God. Thus, shall it be in the day when the Son of man is revealed. When Christ came to gather His Church, many were found in such a state of false security as is here spoken of. In like manner, when Jesus Christ shall come to judge the world, sinners will be found committing sin; for in like manner the sinners of every age go on securely in their evil ways and do not consider their latter end! But wherever the wicked are, who are marked for eternal ruin, they shall be found by the judgments of God.

(E) <u>JESUS DEPICTION OF THE PLACE HE WOULD PREPARE FOR THOSE WHO ARE RAPTURED</u>

(<u>John 14:3</u>) And if I go and prepare a place for you, I will come again, and receive you unto myself; that where I am, there ye may be also.

Jesus promises here that He will come again; the perfect

fulfilment of this promise will be at The Rapture when Christ appeared in the air, when the bodies of believers, being raised in glory, was reunited with their spirits, and they were received by Christ to the everlasting mansions prepared for them in Heaven. But there is also a previous blessed fulfilment to the spirit of each true Christian when he leaves this world. **(See Luke 16:22; 23:43; 2Corinthians 5:8; Revelation 14:13)** I heard Jesus say: I will come again and receive you unto myself. The reference is not to Christ's return from the grave, but to a return from Heaven, the coming of the Lord, which is a part of the Christian faith. **(Compare 1Thessalonians 4:16-17; Philippians 1:23).**

(F)   <u>JESUS ON THE FACT THAT HE IS THE RESURRECTION AND THE LIFE</u>

(John 11:24-26) Martha saith unto him, I know that he shall rise again in the resurrection at the last day. Jesus said unto her, I am the resurrection, and the life: he that believeth in me, though he were dead, yet shall he live: And whosoever liveth and believeth in me shall never die. Believest thou this?

Jesus said to Martha, I am the resurrection; the author of the Resurrection, and the Giver of life. Though Believers were dead; more exactly, though they have died Jesus informed Martha that He can restore someone that believes in Him back to life! The Savior has in mind the case of those who have, like Lazarus, suffered natural death. Though the physical body has died, yet shall he live; his soul shall still live in blessed communion with God! Isn't it amazing that Jesus was revealing that He could call Lazarus' spirit back into that body? To the believer, whose soul is made alive by union with God through Christ, the death of the body will be only a sleep, from which it shall be awakened at the resurrection, to a glorious immortality.

(G)   <u>JESUS SPEAKS THE PARABLE OF THE VIRGINS</u>

(Matthew 25:1-13) Then shall the kingdom of heaven be likened unto ten virgins, which took their lamps, and went forth to meet the

bridegroom. And five of them were wise, and five were foolish. They that were foolish took their lamps and took no oil with them: But the wise took oil in their vessels with their lamps. While the bridegroom tarried, they all slumbered and slept. And at midnight there was a cry made, Behold, the bridegroom cometh; go ye out to meet him. Then all those virgins arose and trimmed their lamps. And the foolish said unto the wise, give us of your oil; for our lamps are gone out. But the wise answered, saying, not so; lest there be not enough for us and you: but go ye rather to them that sell, and buy for yourselves. And while they went to buy, the bridegroom came; and they that were ready went in with him to the marriage: and the door was shut. Afterward came also the other virgins, saying, Lord, Lord, open to us. But he answered and said, Verily I say unto you, I know you not. Watch therefore, for ye know neither the day nor the hour wherein the Son of man cometh.

The time when the Son of man (Jesus) shall come, was foretold in the preceding chapter, Matthew 24, a chapter which gives a descriptive illustration of how the times would be when Jesus was to unexpectedly return! This parable of the Lord Jesus was to occur at The End Of The World and is a depiction of the gathering of His Church or Bride represented here as Ten Virgins, who are supposed to be prepared and waiting on (Jesus), the Bridegroom to come!   The object of this parable is to show that as we did not know when Christ would come, we were instructed to live as to be always ready!   Its highest reference is to His personal coming for a cherished possession, His Bride, who is to remain with Him forever!   Notice in the parable there were Ten Virgins. Five were wise and five were foolish! I want to you to be aware that ALL WERE CONSIDERED VIRGINS, ALL WERE WAITING ON THE BRIDEGROOM!   All in the Church are calling themselves Children of God and all are considering themselves to be Christians, but it seems there are **WISE CHRISTIANS** and there are **FOOLISH CHRISTIANS**! The Foolish were those who took no oil (without oil, one's lamp cannot be lit, without oil one cannot see their way)! The Bridegroom Comes and takes the WISE VIRGINS and shuts the door on the FOOLISH VIRGINS! Notice the doors have been shut on the

Foolish Virgins! In this parable we were warned to **WATCH THEREFORE** for we did not and could not know when the Bridegroom (The Lord) would come or when the Rapture would take place!   My friends, there were numerous parables in the Bible indicating a separation of those who were real in Christ from those who were not: Read: The Parable of the Talents, The Day of Judgment Portrayed, The Gathering of the Nations, The Great Separation of the Sheep from the Goats, The Blessedness of Those on the Right Hand, The Awful Fate of Those on the Left. The Ground of the Separation. The Everlasting Punishment and Life Eternal.

(H)   JESUS SPEAKS THE PARABLE OF THE NET AND THE FISH

(Matthew 13:47-49) Again, the kingdom of heaven is like unto a net, that was cast into the sea, and gathered of every kind: Which, when it was full, they drew to shore, and sat down, and gathered the good into vessels, but cast the bad away. So shall it be at the end of the world: the angels shall come forth, and sever the wicked from among the just, And shall cast them into the furnace of fire: there shall be wailing and gnashing of teeth.

In this parable the Master Jesus says, The Kingdom of Heaven is like a net! The Savior's illustrations all come home to His audience because many of them were fishermen and understood the terminology. Many were husbandmen; many were women familiar with the culinary art; some were merchants; many were fishermen. Jesus speaks of a drag net and the gathering of every kind! Here again, as in the parable of the Tares, it is taught that, at **The End of the World,** the Angels shall sever the wicked from the just! A net--cast into the sea; the sea is the world, and the net is the Gospel with its ministers and ordinances! This parable has a close relation to that of the tares in the field. It shows the mixture of good and evil which will always exist in the visible church (which is not the true church) on earth. We should not be discouraged on account of the mixture of evil with good in God's church; for it has always been so and shall be so to the end of time when the Rapture takes place! It can be of no avail to anyone to be a member of the visible church, unless he or she have also the character of a true Christian! When the net is filled, the fishermen cannot stop to sort while they are drawing the net! Nor can the preachers of the Gospel always distinguish the draw from the Gospel that is preached! So, shall it be at The End of the World when it shall be determined! Then, not men, but the Angels, under the direction of the Son of Man, shall sever the wicked from the just! Then shall the wicked be cast into the furnace of fire! Here is repeated, word for word, the language of **(Matthew 13:42,50).** The tares, the chaff, the corrupt trees, the barren tree, are all represented as burned, and here also the wicked are cast into a furnace. While I suppose that the language is a figure of speech, it can only be understood as indicating that the sufferings of Gehenna, the abode of the wicked, are intense and should be avoided at all costs! **(See also Matthew 8:12)**

(I) <u>JESUS TELLS THE SAINTS THEY WILL NOT SUFFER THE HORRORS OF THE GREAT TRIBULATION</u>

(<u>Revelation 3:10</u>) Because thou hast kept the word of my patience, I also will keep thee from the hour of temptation, which shall come upon all the world, to try them that dwell upon the earth.

Those that were taken in The Rapture, (and I pray I was in that number) did this what the Lord demanded, kept the Word of His patience, and endured many things to stay faithful to Christ in their lifetime on earth! Jesus says, The Raptured, has endured and kept His Word! Planet earth is a trial, and many fail the test of life. But because the true Saints of God have been faithful, Jesus promises to keep them from **The Hour of Temptation**, or Great Tribulation! Yes, Jesus promises to remove His Children from harm's way, in The Rapture, that His Children will not endure what is coming upon the earth! Now, there shall be a stern and cruel trial for the earth….- The Time of Jacobs Trouble, The Great Tribulation and as the Bible says - The End of the Age! Now a great crisis of trial and sorrow is to come on all the world! It is an hour of temptation, a season of fiery trial, apparently in the shape of severe sorrows! We may not know just what our Lord referred to, but we can believe that He fulfilled His promise. The Lord's coming is promised in **(Revelation 2:25; 3:3)**! In the first instance it is said He will come; in a second, as a thief; but here, that He will come quickly.

(J) <u>JESUS TELLS THE SAINTS HE WILL REMOVE THEM FROM GREAT TRIBULATION</u>

(Revelation 2:25) But that which ye have already hold fast till I come.
(<u>Revelation 3:3</u>) Remember therefore how thou hast received and heard, and hold fast, and repent. If therefore thou shalt not watch, I will come on thee as a thief, and thou shalt not know what hour I will come upon thee.

This parable depicts a promise that Jesus made to His Church and since The Rapture has occurred, it has come to pass! Jesus Himself warned all to hold fast! He warned all to hold to the Gospel as it has been taught to you. He warned to hold to the true Gospel from the elders who were established in the faith! Jesus warned His people to remember! Remember the teaching formerly received, cling to it, and repent of the falling away from it! In these end times many have strayed from the Gospel of Christ and given in to another gospel that wasn't taught by Jesus, the Apostles nor your ancestors who passed it down their bloodlines! Do you remember how you received and heard from the elders, your grandparents, those who were dedicated to God; the blessings bestowed, and the truths inspired upon them to you, they passed it on, why should one turn from it? Jesus warned that He would come as a thief; suddenly and unexpectedly! I will come on thee as a thief. Suddenly, in a sudden judgment and for that reason the warning was for you to be ready!

CHAPTER 7
OTHERS BELIEVED IN THE RAPTURE?

WHAT THIS CHAPTER IS ABOUT
IN THE PREVIOUS CHAPTER 6 NOT ONLY DID JESUS PREDICT THE RAPTURE OF
THE CHRISTIAN CHURCH AND BELEIVERS THAT HAD DIED SINCE ADAM, BUT IN
THIS CHAPTER THE APOSTLE PAUL, PETER, LUKE, JOHN, JUDE, AND EVEN
MOSES ALL SPOKE ON THE EVENT!   THEY WARNED THAT JESUS WOULD COME
AND GATHER HIS PEOPLE AND THOUGH THEY WERE DEAD, YET SHALL THEY
LIVE, AND THOSE THAT ARE ALIVE SHALL BE TAKEN ALONG WITH THEM!

I want to start with Paul's teachings on The Rapture because
the revelation or mystery of many of the details pertaining to The
Rapture were revealed by The Holy Spirit through Paul!
Understand that **The Rapture is the 2nd Phase of The First
Resurrection** (That study of the First Resurrection is in Chapter
11) and it is the phase where Jesus is gathering The Church and all
the Saints or Believers from Adam to The Church to take them to
a Heavenly Paradise!   Let's look at what The Apostle Paul and
others had to say on this subject.

(A)   PAUL SPEAKS OF SUFFERINGS THAT CANNOT COMPARE TO THE GLORY WHEN RAPTURED

*(Romans 8:18-19) For I reckon that the sufferings of this present
time are not worthy to be compared with the glory which shall be
revealed in us. For the earnest expectation of the creature waiteth
for the manifestation of the sons of God.*

The sufferings of this present time; that Christians were
asked to endure in this world were a small task!   Those Christians
will tell you that the things they suffered were not worthy to be
compared; 9was very small, as nothing in comparison).to what they
have obtained in Glory—or the Glory revealed in them now that
we have been raptured out by Christ **(See Ephesians 3:16-19;
Colossians 3:4; 2Thessalonians 1:10; 1John 3:2)**!   I am told to

tell you that all sacrifices which men make to obey God and all trials that they are called to endure, are light and momentary, compared with the blessings which He will bestow upon them in Heaven!

The sufferings of this present time are nothing, temporal. The Christians of our time have little conception of the sufferings of the ancient Saints, counted as outcasts, despised, persecuted, and slain **(See Romans 8:36; also, 2Corinthians 11:23-28**). Yet Paul counted these as nothing in view of the hope of eternal glory. All the Saints that were taken in The Rapture view the sacrifices they made for Christ the same! But those left behind avoided sufferings that they may stay acceptable to a world that was ruled by Satan and the forces of evil.

Revealed in us. In the Saints when they shall have received the inheritance which God bestows in Christ. The comforts of the Saints during suffering are now given: (1) The hope of glory for which all creation, ruined by the Fall, is looking. (2) The present help of the Spirit. (3) The overruling providence of God.

The creature; the creation. In this and the three following verses the word rendered creature and creation is the same in the original Greek. It seems to denote the whole of this lower creation as brought under God's curse and made subject to suffering and abuse in connection with the fall of man. (**Compare Genesis 3:16-19)**. The manifestation of the sons of God; when they shall be seen and publicly acknowledged as His children and take full possession of their inheritance as heirs of God, and joint heirs with Christ. The whole creations of God are represented as earnestly looking forward to that day of future glory when the sons of God will have reached their high estate and be revealed as His children. It is a fine, poetic figure: a grand conception!

(B) <u>PAUL SPOKE OF THE MYSTERY OF THE</u>

<u>RAPTURE!</u>

(<u>1 Corinthians 15:51-58</u>) Behold, I shew you a mystery; We shall not all sleep, but we shall all be changed, In a moment, in the twinkling of an eye, at the last trump: for the trumpet shall sound, and the dead shall be raised incorruptible, and we shall be changed. For this corruptible must put on incorruption, and this mortal must put on immortality. For this corruptible must put on incorruption, and this mortal must put on immortality. So, when this corruptible shall have put on incorruption, and this mortal shall have put on immortality, then shall be brought to pass the saying that is written, Death is swallowed up in victory. O death, where is thy sting? O grave, where is thy victory? The sting of death is sin; and the strength of sin is the law. But thanks be to God, which giveth us the victory through our Lord Jesus Christ. Therefore, my beloved brethren, be ye steadfast, unmovable, always abounding in the work of the Lord, forasmuch as ye know that your labor is not in vain in the Lord.

<u>Behold, I tell you a mystery.</u> I disclose to you a secret of which you have had, no knowledge!

<u>We shall not all sleep!</u>   Not all true Christians will sleep or will have died physical deaths when Jesus returns! I want you to understand that the Christians who have died and the Christians who are still alive are the ones Jesus has come to retrieve!   There will be some on the earth who shall be alive when Christ comes! These Christians who shall be living (alive) at the time of The Rapture**,** and have not died, will experience the same change as the ones who have died! All or both will experience resurrection change or transformation, becoming spiritual, incorruptible, and immortal!

<u>For this incorruptible.</u> All shall be made immortal and incorruptible. For this corruptible body must give place to the incorruptible body; the mortal frame to an immortal one. One must be put off, the other put on. **(See 2Corinthians 5:2).** Then, when the dead have been raised, and the living so changed as to fit them to live and reign with Christ!   The saying: shall be fulfilled that is written in **(Isa 25:8).** Then shall be brought to pass the saying Death is swallowed up in victory! This is the final victory, the victory over death. O death, where is thy sting? This is quoted from **(Hosea 13:14).**   It is here the triumphant shout of the Apostle is made as he sees by faith the final victory over death! The sting of death; that which makes death terrible, is sin **(Romans 4:15; 6:23).** The sting of death is sin. It is sin that gives death his power to sting and destroy. **(See Romans 6:23).**   The power of sin is the law. The law, broken, is sin, and when this law is consciously broken the conscience is wounded. When a moral law is broken, moral death follows. If there was no law of any kind, there would be no sin, no wounded consciences, no moral death **(See Romans 7:7).** Thanks be to God for the victory over sin and death through Christ.

(1Corinthians 15:58) Therefore, my beloved brethren, be ye steadfast, unmovable, always abounding in the work of the Lord, forasmuch as ye know that your labor is not in vain in the Lord!

(C) PAUL SPOKE OF HOW THE RAPTURE OF THE SAINTS WILL HAPPEN

(1 Thessalonians 4:16-17) For the Lord Himself shall descend from Heaven with a shout, with the voice of the Archangel, and with the trump of God: and the dead in Christ shall rise first: Then we which are alive and remain shall be caught up together with them in the clouds, to meet the Lord in the air: and so shall we ever be with the Lord. Wherefore comfort one another with these words.

The change was instantaneous! At the last trump, the trumpet shall sound **(See 1Corinthians 15:52).**   This signal is for the close of all earthly things. And the Saints of God were changed! For the Lord Himself descended from Heaven with a shout with the voice of an archangel and with the voice of command and with the trump of God!   The trumpet blast was a signal and a summons! You would have thought that **The Living Saints** would hurry to meet the Lord, and that the dead would be powerless to follow! On the contrary, Paul conveys through the Word of God that there is an order of retrieval, Christ came and gathered **The Departed Saints** first, then The Living Saints!

NOTE: I WANT YOU TO UNDERSTAND THAT WHEN THE BIBLE SAYS THE DEAD IN CHRIST IT IS SPEAKING OF THE DEAD BODIES OF THE SAINTS THAT LIE IN DUST! THE LORD COMES TO RETRIEVE THEIR BODIES, FOR THEIR SPIRITS (OR SOULS) COME WITH THE LORD THAT THEY MAY RE-ENTER THEIR BODIES TO HAVE THEIR MORTAL BODIED CHANGED OR GLORIFIED!

So, before the living are gathered, all the Saints who slept in Christ shall be gathered around Him, in other words, their spirits are gathered around Christ to meet their retrieved bodies! In The Rapture, the first act is the gathering of The Departed Saints; the next, will be the gathering of The Living Saints! Understand that Christ, who comes in the air of the atmosphere, returns with the spirits of The Departed Saints whose bodies lie in the grave!   The Departed Saints have waited in the Heavenly Paradise for the event of The Rapture, when Christ would retrieve their deceased bodies! The Living Saints will be raised after the bodies of the Departed Saints are raised to meet Christ in the air, and all are instantly glorified!   So, that you truly understand what happened when The Rapture took place; the dead in Christ were risen first; then the living and all were changed!   Then both ascended together with Christ to be forever with the Lord.

(D)   PAUL REVEALED HOW THE BODIES OF THOSE TAKEN IN THE RAPTURE WERE CHANGED

> *(Philippians 3:20-21) For our conversation is in heaven; from whence also we look for the Savior, the Lord Jesus Christ: Who shall change our vile body, that it may be fashioned like unto His glorious body, according to the working whereby He is able even to subdue all things unto Himself.*

What I want you to understand is that the conversation of the true Christians, who have been raptured, was centered on Heaven not the things of the evil world. That was our citizenship. We considered ourselves to be citizens of Heaven itself, Heaven was our country though we were on earth!   While we were on earth, we considered ourselves to be absent from our homeland and we were always seeking to return! So, our mind was always on Heavenly things. There our Lord dwells, and from there we knew He would come!   Yes, true Christians knew our citizenship: that we are citizens of Heaven; we knew our King, Jesus resided there; our hearts and thoughts were there; we obeyed its laws and looked to it as our everlasting home!   As Christians are citizens of Heaven, we knew we were only pilgrims and sojourners here, and that is why we were not greatly influenced by things of earth, or chiefly occupied with its concerns. Our treasures and hearts were Heaven-focused; and we looked to Christ to change us into His own glorious image and raise us to forever reign with Him in the Kingdom of GOD!   The Lord, as promised, came in the Rapture and changed our vile bodies!   He said He would change, at The Rapture, our lowly body causing it to undergo a change to fit it for Heaven! It then took the form of His glorified body, such as was seen at the Transfiguration. **(Compare 1Corinthians 15:43-52)**

> ***(2Corinthians 5:1-4)**; For we know that if our earthly house of this tabernacle were dissolved, we have a building of God, a house not made with hands, eternal in the Heavens. For in this we groan, earnestly desiring to be clothed upon with our house which is from Heaven: If so, be that being clothed we shall not be found naked. For we that are in this tabernacle do groan, being burdened: not for that we would be unclothed, but clothed upon, that mortality might be swallowed up of life.*

and

> ***(1John 3:2)** Beloved, now are we the Sons of God, and it doth not yet appear what we shall be: but we know that, when He shall appear, we shall be like Him; for we shall see Him as He is.*

The Apostle Paul in this scripture shows what it takes to come to Christ and totally depend on Him. Notice: this simple dependence and earnestness of soul, was not mentioned as if the Apostle had gained the prize or was already made perfect in the

Savior's likeness. He forgot the things which were behind, so as not to be content with past labors or present measures of grace. He reached forth, stretched himself forward towards his point; expressions showing great concern to become more and more like unto Christ. Eternal life is the gift of God, but it is in Christ Jesus; through His hand it must come to you, as it is procured for you by Him. There is no getting to Heaven as your home, but by Christ as your Way. True believers, in seeking this assurance, as well as to glorify Him, will seek more nearly to resemble His sufferings and death, by dying to sin, and by crucifying the flesh with its affections and lusts. In these things there is a great difference among real and false Christians, but all know something of what it takes, some just do not perform it. Believers make Christ all in all and set their hearts upon another world. If they differ from one another and are not of the same judgment in lesser matters, they all meet now in-Christ, and many have met in Heaven.   The enemies of the cross of Christ minded nothing but their sensual appetites. Sin is the sinner's shame, especially when gloried in. The way of those who mind earthly things, may seem pleasant, but death and hell are at the end of it. If you choose their way, you shall share their end.

(E)   <u>PAUL REVEALS THE JUDGMENT SEAT OF CHRIST</u>

<u>(2 Corinthians 5:10)</u> For we must all appear before the Judgment Seat of Christ; that every one may receive the things done in his body, according to that he hath done, whether it be good or bad.

For we must all appear before **The Judgment Seat of Christ,** which will occur immediately after The Rapture of the Church when the Saints are translated to Heaven. This is a stimulus to Saints to labor to be accepted by Christ **(2Corinthians 5:9).** The object of this judgment is that a Saint may reap the fruits of what he/she has done in the body when he/she stands before **The Judgment Seat of Christ.** The language here implies that our probation ends with our earthly life! An abiding conviction that each individual will stand at The Judgment Seat of Christ, **and** receive according to the deeds done in the body, is adapted to make Saints careful, and lead them most earnestly to desire and diligently labor that they may be accepted of Jesus and that the work done for **the** Kingdom of God in this life is worthy of eternal reward!

(F)   <u>PETER COMPARES THE DAYS OF NOAH TO THE RAPTURE</u>

> ***(1Peter 3:20)*** ***Which sometime were disobedient, when once the longsuffering of God waited in the days of Noah, while the ark was a preparing, wherein few, that is, eight souls were saved by water.***

The long-suffering of God waited in the days of Noah. They that were in the world had then refused to obey the call to repentance. It is stated in **(Genesis 6:3)** that the long suffering of God waited 120 years. Even the inhabitants of the world rejected the message of Noah, eight souls were saved from the destruction that followed! This difficult passage has been given two interpretations. The more common view is that Jesus, after His suffering and physical death on the cross, during the interval before His resurrection, went without His body (which laid in the tomb) in a spirit form, to these antediluvians (early inhabitants of planet earth) and preached to them in the prison house of Hell where their spirits were confined! If this view is correct, it only teaches that an offer of salvation was then made to these disobedient ones, who were given an opportunity, who had never before heard of Christ, before their pending final judgment would come at the end of age! This was part of the First Phase of **The First Resurrection** that Jesus performed before He ascended to Heaven! It furnishes no comfort to those that have an opportunity after knowing of Christ and reject it in this life. It only shows that one opportunity is given to all. The other view is that Christ went in spirit in the person of Noah and by him preached to those who were afterwards held in prison on account of their disobedience. The first view seems more in harmony with the context; the second furnishes fewer theological difficulties. I, accept the first view, believing that Christ Himself entered the confines of Hell as the King of Glory and offered the captives deliverance if they accepted Him! Isn't it something that so few were saved in the Days of Noah?

Wherein few, that is, eight souls!   Only eight souls out of a great multitude were saved; these were saved through water, since it bore up the ark. The [Greek] word [dia] rendered through, means by means of.

Which sometime were disobedient; when they were alive on the earth, and Christ, by Noah, preached to them during the building of the ark. Wherein, in the ark. eight souls; Noah and his wife, his three sons and their wives. **(Genesis 7:7).**

Were saved; through believing and obeying God, preparing an ark and entering it. By water; by the instrumentality of water. The water which destroyed the wicked bore up the ark and floated it in safety. The idea that the apostle Peter, or any other writer of the Holy Scriptures, teaches that there is such a place or state as purgatory, is false and pernicious, for one must accept salvation in this physical life or lose eternal glory with God!

(G)   <u>LUKE, JUDE, AND PETER COMPARED THE END OF TIME WILL BE AS THE DAYS OF LOT</u>

> *(<u>Luke 17:28-30)</u>   Likewise also as it was in the days of Lot; they did eat, they drank, they bought, they sold, they planted, they builded; But the same day that Lot went out of Sodom it rained fire and brimstone from Heaven, and destroyed them all.   Even thus shall it be in the day when the Son of man is revealed.*

The utterance of the Lord Jesus, likewise also as it was in the days of Lot, indicates that these End of Days will be the same, the reemergence of rampant homosexuality as never seen before, which is a sure sign that **The End of Time** has come! This saturation is an open rebellion against the Will and Word of The Most High! Even as Sodom and Gomorrah.

(2Peter 2:6) And turning the cities of Sodom and Gomorrah into ashes condemned them with an overthrow, making them an ensample unto those that after should live ungodly;

And what did God do for Lot who was caught in the midst of the homosexual environment? God delivered righteous Lot who was vexed, upset and disturbed by the lifestyle of the homosexuals: he was not open and acceptable as this sinful world is! The saving of the righteous or the calling out of God's people is as marked as a sure that the punishment of the wicked, shall follow!

(Jude 1:7) Even as Sodom and Gomorrah, and the cities about them in like manner, giving themselves over to fornication, and going after strange flesh, are set forth for an example, suffering the vengeance of eternal fire.
(2Peter 2:10) But chiefly them that walk after the flesh in the lust of uncleanness, and despise government. Presumptuous are they, self-willed, they are not afraid to speak evil of dignities.

We are living in a time when sin is rampant and there are many who go after the flesh! Many in these end times follow its dictates and live impure lives! Many despise government and refuse to submit to authority, even the authority of God! They are not afraid to speak evil of dignities! A characteristic of this class is their arrogance and desire to be respected but not giving respect to those appointed by God to give them truth and light **(See Jude 1:8)!**

But chiefly them; these are the individuals, unjust, just spoken of. Lot was a Godly man, but when he spoke to his sons-in-law about leaving Sodom, he was mocked by them, treated with disrespect, they did not believe what he said. Being who he was, should not Lot have been treated with respect and obeyed **(Genesis 19:14)?** These were individuals, unjust, just spoken of.

The end time world is the same, harboring a disrespect for those who are leaders appointed by God but honoring those that lead it to damnation!

As in the Days of Lot and of Noah, for their **d**ebauchery, sensuality, or depravity, terrible destruction came upon them. Suffering the vengeance of eternal fire, they are to be cast into endless perdition with the devil and his angels **(Matthew 25:41).** Of this the flames which consumed their cities and made them desolate forever were a solemn symbol **(Genesis 19:24-25).** The destruction of the inhabitants of Sodom, and of the angels that sinned with Lucifer and those who left their first estate, is recorded for the warning of sinners in all ages, and to show that however great the blessings men may enjoy, if they reject the Gospel, or continue in sin, they will inevitably and awfully perish!

Outward privileges, profession, and apparent conversion could not secure those from the vengeance of God, who turned aside in unbelief and disobedience! The destruction of the unbelieving Israelites in the wilderness, shows that none ought to presume on their privileges. They had miracles as their daily bread; yet even they perished in unbelief. A great number of the angels were not pleased with the stations God allotted to them; pride was the main and direct cause or occasion of their fall. The fallen angels are kept to the judgment of the great day; and shall fallen men escape it? Surely not. Consider this in due time. The destruction of Sodom is a loud warning to all, to take heed of, and flee from fleshly lusts that war against the soul, **(1Peter 2:11).** God is the same holy, just, pure being now, as then. Stand in awe, therefore, and sin not, **(Psalms 4:4).** Let us not rest in anything that does not make the soul subject to the obedience of Christ; for nothing but the renewal of our souls to the Divine image by the Holy Spirit can keep us from being destroyed among the enemies of God. If God judges angels, how then should man tremble, who drinks iniquity like water!

(H)   LUKE SPEAKS OF LOT'S WIFE AS A PERFECT EXAMPLE OF THOSE LEFT BEHIND IN THE RAPTURE

(Luke 17:32-33) Remember Lot's wife.   Whosoever shall seek to save his life shall lose it; and whosoever shall lose his life shall preserve it.

Lot's wife; lost her life by disobeying God's command, not to look back **(Genesis 19:17,26).** There are many who professed Christ who did as she did, look back to where she had come. Looked back because there was a longing for the old life, and things of the past! Looked back because she did not want to go where God was leading her, despite the evilness and filth of sin she was leaving behind, she still desires that atmosphere, that situation, that condition!   So, those who do not follow Christ's directions will perish! Remember that Lot's wife, by tarrying and looking back, lost her life **(Genesis 19:15-17,26).**   So hesitation and delay at this great crisis that you now face, being left behind by Christ, will be perilous to your eternal future if you disobey the directives I shall give you to still have a last possibility to be saved! . If you shall seek to save your temporal, physical, fleshly life, you shall lose it by being ultimately cast in the Lake of Fire with the devil and his angels **(Matthew 10:39).** Seeking to save the physical, earthly, fleshly life along with gratifying the flesh; by disobeying the will of Christ leads to destruction!

(I)   PAUL COMPARED ENOCH TO A TYPE OF RAPTURED SAINT THAT DID NOT SEE DEATH

(Hebrews 11:5) By faith Enoch was translated that he should not see death; and was not found, because God had translated him: for before his translation he had this testimony, that he pleased God.

The Bible reveals that Enoch was a type of Raptured Saint! By faith Enoch was translated or Raptured **(See Genesis 5:24; also, Jude 1:14).**   The Bible explicitly reveals his character and faithfulness of life to God and why God looked upon him with extreme favor. His faithfulness was rewarded by a translation to Heaven without first becoming a victim of death.   Enoch's life created an atmosphere that people talked about or testified about! Regarding Enoch, people had this testimony: The testimony is that he walked with God, and God took him, because He was pleased with him. He pleased God; by walking with Him **(Genesis 5:24).** He had confidence in him, lived in communion with Him, opened his heart to Him, and consulted Him as his bosom-friend. So, God took him without him having to taste death, this is the disposition of all the Saints who are faithful to God and who love God and put Him first in their lives!! Yes, Enoch was an Old Testament living Raptured Child of God!

(J) <u>MOSES COMPARED ENOCH TO A TYPE OF RAPTURED SAINT THAT DID NOT SEE DEATH</u>

(Genesis 5:24)   And Enoch walked with God: and he was not; for God took him.

Moses was the writer of the Book of Genesis, but he knew of Enoch! Moses told us that Enoch was the seventh from Adam who was known for a godly walk with God! For one to walk with God one must submit to God having a spirit of reconciliation to God!. Enoch illustrated a godly, righteous, and sober life. To walk with God, is to set God always before us, to act as always under His eye. Enoch lived his life wanting to take care, in all things to please God!   The Holy Spirit, instead of saying, Enoch lived, says, Enoch walked with God!   Enoch was removed to a better world. As he did not live like the rest of mankind, so he did not leave the world by death as they did.

He was not found, because God had translated him, **(Hebrews 11:5).** He had lived but 365 years, which, as men's ages were then, was but the midst of a man's days. Enoch's removal is expressed: **<u>HE WAS NOT</u>**, for God took him! He was not any longer in this world; he was changed, as the Saints shall be, who are alive; Christ shall Rapture them!   The true Christian's walk in holiness, through many a year, is steady till God takes him!   And walking with God well agrees with the cares, comforts, and duties of life.   To walk with God is the highest duty, the greatest honor, excellence, and blessedness of man. **(See Jude 1:14-15; Hebrews 11:5-6).**

(K)   <u>JUDE QUOTED THE BOOK OF ENOCH WHO SAW JESUS COMING WITH THE RAPTURED SAINTS</u>

> ***(Jude 1:14-15)*** *And Enoch also, the seventh from Adam, prophesied of these, saying, Behold, the Lord cometh with ten thousands of his saints, To execute judgment upon all, and to convince all that are ungodly among them of all their ungodly deeds which they have ungodly committed, and of all their hard speeches which ungodly sinners have spoken against him.*

And Enoch also was a prophet, for God revealed many things to him about the End Times. This prophecy of the holiest man of the antediluvian world might have been preserved by tradition. It is found in the Book of Enoch, a work long lost, but recovered in modern times in Abyssinia, supposed to have been composed the century before Christ. Wherever Jude met it, he was familiar with the prophecy. The seventh from Adam. To the Jew there was a sacredness in seven. To execute judgment upon all. For a general judgment. To convince. To convict all ungodly men of their ungodly deeds. Yes, Enoch saw, by the Holy Spirit, The Second Coming of The Lord Jesus Christ with the Raptured Saints to execute judgment an ungodly world!

CHAPTER 8
THE SPIRITUAL LAW OF OBEDIENCE

WHAT THIS CHAPTER IS ABOUT
JESUS, THE APOSTLE PAUL AND PROPHETS SPOKE OF THE RAPTURE IN CHAPTERS 6 & 7 NOW I AM TAKING A TURN AWAY FROM PROVING THE CERTAINTY OF THE RAPTURE TO EXAMINE WITH YOU THAT IN ORDER TO HAVE A RELATIONSHIP WITH GOD, OBEDIENCE TO GOD, IS OF VITAL IMPORTANCE! IN THIS CHAPTER I WILL LOOK AT (4) MAJOR HOLY MEN THAT SPOKE ON THE SUBJECT AND I PRAY THAT YOU WILL BE ABLE TO SEE WHY IT IS NECESSARY FOR YOU TO TRUST AND OBEY GOD IN THIS DARK HOUR OF GREAT TRIBULATION SO THAT YOU MAY BE SAVED IN THE END!

THE HOLY SPIRIT THROUGH PAUL SPEAKS ON OBEDIENCE TO GOD

(Romans 6:16) says: Know ye not, that to whom ye yield yourselves servants to obey, his servants ye are to whom ye obey; whether of sin unto death, or of obedience unto righteousness?.

I thought I would put this here regarding the spiritual law of obedience and how it determines whether one is serving God or Satan.   I think it is appropriate after studying the information regarding The Great Tribulation, The Resurrection & The Rapture and showing the sentence of judgment on Satan and his fallen angels, along with wicked men and women!   This chapter should cause you to desire a clearer picture of the exact things you must do to become aligned with God   Every person who has been blessed to experience individual life on this planet daily chooses the service of self and sin, or of Christ and holiness. One leads to life, the other to death.   God sets both options before men, and invites them to choose life by taking the way which leads to it, and promises that if they do, they shall live. (**Deuteronomy 30:19; Joshua 24:15**). If we obey sin, we are sin's servants, under Satan's reign who is the father of sin, and will receive, not grace, but sin's wages, which is death!   On the other hand, if we obey Christ, we are His servants, and enjoy His righteousness. **None enjoy this blessedness but those who turn from sin and obey Christ.** We are servants to whom we obey! And though you find yourself in The Great Tribulation, and the true Christian Church has been Raptured, **God is still demanding that you willfully choose to obey Him, even now, regardless of the cost you must now pay, can you do that???**

THE HOLY SPIRIT THROUGH MOSES SPEAKS ON OBEDIENCE TO GOD

(Deuteronomy 30:19)   I call heaven and earth to record this day against you, that I have set before you - life and death, blessing and cursing: therefore choose life, that both thou and thy seed may live:

What could be said more moving of a choice, and more likely to make deep and lasting impressions? Every man wishes to obtain life and blessings, and to escape death and evil; he desires happiness, and dreads misery. So great is the compassion of the Lord, that He has favored men, by His Word, with such a knowledge of good and evil as will make them forever happy, we get to choose. Let us hear the sum of the whole matter. If they and theirs would love God, and serve Him, they should live and be happy. If they or theirs should turn from God, desert His service, and worship other gods, that would certainly be their ruin. There never was, since the fall of man, more than one way to Heaven, which is marked out in both Testaments, though not with equal clearness. Moses meant that same way of acceptance, which Paul more plainly described; and Paul's words mean the same obedience, on which Moses more fully treated. In both Testaments the good and right way is brought near, and plainly revealed to us and it is simply: **Will you obey God and live eternally???**

THE HOLY SPIRIT THROUGH JOSHUA SPEAKS ON OBEDIENCE TO GOD

(Joshua 24:15) And if it seem evil unto you to serve the LORD, choose you this day whom ye will serve; whether the gods which your fathers served that were on the other side of the flood, or the gods of the Amorites, in whose land ye dwell: but as for me and my house, we will serve the LORD.

True Christianity is a matter of choice with all who heartily embrace it, and no man ever does or can serve God, in spirit and in truth, without choosing to do so. But no one can come to God except God draws them! The fact that you are reading this book indicates that God is drawing you to Himself, but you must make the choice to submit to Him! Of course ministers can present to men the motives which are best suited to lead them to do this, and I pray their preaching should add the influence of their example! I am a preacher, attempting to enlighten you so you can understand the choices available to you! Why do men and women act as if they are doubtful whether Jehovah or Baal were the true God? As Jehovah has in various ways shown conclusively that He is the only living and true God, I would reason that all to whom He is revealed to should, without hesitation or reserve, love, worship, and obey Him! The commands of God are reasonable and binding on all who know them. If men do not obey them, it is because they have no disposition to obey.

THE HOLY SPIRIT THROUGH THE PROPHET SAMUEL SPEAKS ON OBEDIENCE TO GOD

(1Samuel 15:22) And Samuel said, Hath the LORD as great delight in burnt offerings and sacrifices, as in obeying the voice of the LORD? Behold, to obey is better than sacrifice, and to hearken than the fat of rams.

No external attention, even to things which God has commanded, can be accepted as a substitute for an obedient heart! For God is a Spirit, and to be accepted, men must obey Him in spirit and in truth. In these ends of days many have diverted from the truth of God's commands and have disobeyed and felt it was alright with God to do things their way! I wish you to look at what Saul did after he had been commanded to slay utterly all the Amalekites and their cattle. Instead of doing so, he preserved the Amalekite king, and suffered his people to take the best of the oxen and of the sheep. When called to account for this, he declared that he did it with a view of offering sacrifice to God; but Samuel met him at once with the assurance that sacrifices were no excuse for an act of direct rebellion and disobedience to the command of God.

The sentence before us is worthy to be printed in letters of gold, and to be hung up before the eyes of this present End of the Age idolatrous generation , who are very fond of the fineries of self-indulgence and false worship, but utterly neglect the Word and Will of God. Be it ever in your remembrance, that to keep strictly in the path of your Savior's command is better than any outward form of religion; and to hearken to His commands with an attentive ear is better than to bring the fat of rams, or any other precious thing to lay upon His altar. If you are failing to keep the least of Christ's commands while claiming to be His disciple, I pray you be disobedient no longer!   All the pretensions you make of your attachment to Jesus and the Church and all the devout actions which you may perform, are no recompense for disobedience! **To obey, even in the slightest and smallest thing, is better than sacrifice,** however pompous! Talk not of the Gospel songs you sing, or your recital of the Lord's teachings, for all your formalities have profited you nothing, for you have been left behind by Christ! It is a blessed thing to be teachable as a little child, but it is a much more blessed thing when one has been taught the lesson, to carry it out to the letter. How many have magnified the beauty of their temples and decorate their Pastors with honors but refuse to obey the Word of the Lord!

THE HOLY SPIRIT THROUGH THE LORD JESUS CHRIST SPEAKS ON OBEDIENCE TO GOD

(John 14:15)   In fact, Jesus said, If you love me, you will obey what I command.
(John 15:10) If ye keep my commandments, ye shall abide in my love; even as I have kept my Father's commandments, and abide in his love.

Jesus said: **If ye love Me, keep My commandments.** Keeping the commandments will be the result if we love Him. The Revised Version gives the true idea (If ye love me, ye will keep my commandments). Obedience is the fruit of love.   Jesus makes it even more clear by saying, **if ye keep my commandments, ye shall abide in my love.**   He abides in the love of the Father by a life of perfect obedience. So, shall we abide in His love if we keep His commandments! So, what is Jesus saying? I think He is saying if we truly love God, we will keep His commandments, we will obey His Word and His will, and obedience to Christ proves that! If we are not willing to obey the will and Word of God, it proves that we do not truly love God!   Jesus proved His love for the Father, and for us, by laying down His life: **Greater love hath no man than this, that a man lay down his life for his friends.** The highest human exhibition of love that earth has ever seen was this. Christ exhibited this highest type of human love by dying for his friends which is a noble thing to do! But Jesus did even more, as Paul shows us in **(Romans 5:6), HE DIED FOR HIS ENEMIES**, never had a man done that!

CHAPTER 9
THINGS THAT DO NOT MAKE YOU A CHRISTIAN

WHAT THIS CHAPTER IS ABOUT
NOW, I WISH TO EXAMINE YOUR BELIEFS, BECAUSE IN THEM LIE THE REASON YOU WERE LEFT BEHIND BY CHRIST!   I PRAY THAT YOU WILL BE OPEN TO NOT ONLY EXAMINE WHAT YOU BELIEVE BUT BE ABLE TO ACKNOWLEDGE THE TRUTHS OF THE POSSIBILITY THAT WHAT YOU WERE BELIEVING WASN'T VALID! THE THINGS I WILL BRING UP MAY HELP IDENTIFY THE REASON YOU WERE LEFT BEHIND!   THERE IS RESOLUTION IN KNOWING THE REASON(S)!   KNOWING THE REASON(S) WILL SETTLE YOUR QUESTIONS AND MISGIVINGS, AND ENABLE US TO MOVE FORWARD TO SEEK ANOTHER SOLUTION TO YOUR DILEMMA!

I know that it is shocking to realize that The Lord Jesus Christ has gathered His Church and left you behind, and you are probably asking yourself - **WHY?**   I know that many who have be left behind believed that they were Christians, and you were probably one of them!   If you were, did you really believe you were a "true Christian" or were you just someone professing Christianity? What I mean by that is: were you someone who was not a true Christian and knew it?   This is important for you to grasp, so that you can examine the area(s) where you fell short.   Evidently, the Lord Jesus did not feel you were ready for Glory and that you were none of His, for He knows His sheep, and His sheep follow Him! Maybe you were left behind because of a lack of understanding or lack of knowledge regarding the Will and Word of God!   I ask these questions and say these things not to hurt you but to cause you to look at possibilities!   For I do not know specifically why Jesus did not translate you in **The Rapture,** but I do know you need to understand that **there was a reason!**   It is necessary for you to understand the mistakes and the misconceptions you had regarding Christianity, for I want you to understand the importance of knowing what true Christianity is! Don't be discouraged or dismayed, just be determined to do what you must do as we progress forward!   In Chapters 5, 15,16 & 17, I will show you, through the Holy Spirit, that there is still **ONE LAST OPPORTUNITY FOR YOU TO MAKE IT TO HEAVEN**! So, let us begin to peel away the deceptions the enemy and the forces of evil has placed in the minds of many that professed Christianity so that you get a firm idea of why you weren't taken!

I am reminded of what the Apostle Paul said to Israel in:

> **(<u>Romans 10:1-3</u>)   Brethren, my heart's desire and prayer to God for Israel is, that they might be saved. For I bear them record that they have a zeal of God, <u>but not according to knowledge.</u> For they being ignorant of God's righteousness, and going about to establish their own righteousness, have not submitted themselves unto the righteousness of God.**

That is my prayer for you, that we can establish the knowledge required that you may understand what God's requirements was and how God now wants you to submit to **The Righteousness of God**!

<u>THESE THINGS DO NOT MAKE YOU CHRISTIAN</u>

Now I am going to throw some light on <u>misconceptions about Christianity</u> that the enemy has deceived many to believe, causing them to be rejected by Jesus when He came to gather His Church in **The Rapture!**   Maybe these false beliefs are some of the errors that caused you to be rejected by Christ and be left behind!   Let us look at these **THINGS THAT DO NOT MAKE YOU A CHRISTIAN** and please consider each one carefully because some of these beliefs and activities you may have been deceived to believe as truth, when in reality, they are all **spiritual error!:**

Just to say, '<u>I believed in God</u>,' **DOES NOT** make you a Christian or get you to Heaven!
Just saying '<u>I am a Christian</u>,' **DOES NOT** make you a Christian or get you to Heaven!
Just because you <u>attend church services</u>, **DOES NOT**

make you a Christian or get you to Heaven!

Having your <u>name on a church membership</u>, **DOES NOT** make you a Christian or get you to Heaven!

Repeating the <u>sinner's prayer without repenting</u>, **DOES NOT** make you a Christian or get you to Heaven!

Just being <u>baptized or sprinkled</u>, **DOES NOT** make you a Christian or get you to Heaven!

<u>Paying tithes</u>, **DOES NOT** make you a Christian or get you to Heaven!

<u>Denominational affiliation</u>, **DOES NOT** make you a Christian or get you to Heaven!

Doing <u>good deeds</u>, **DOES NOT** make you a Christian or get you to Heaven!

<u>Loving the world and things of the world</u>, **DOES NOT** make you a Christian or get you to Heaven!

<u>Giving</u> to and <u>servicing the poor and needy</u>, **DOES NOT** make you a Christian or get you to Heaven!

<u>Claiming be a Christian while living a sinful lifestyle</u>, **DOES NOT** make you a Christian or get you to Heaven!

<u>Helping the underprivileged</u>, **DOES NOT** make you a Christian or get you to Heaven!

Performing <u>missionary work</u>, **DOES NOT** make you a Christian or get you to Heaven!

Performing <u>church-related services</u>, **DOES NOT** make you a Christian or get you to Heaven!

<u>Volunteer work</u>, **DOES NOT** make you a Christian or get you to Heaven!

Being <u>a good and decent person</u>, **DOES NOT** make you a Christian or get you to Heaven!

Being a <u>leader in the church</u>, **DOES NOT** make you a Christian or get you to Heaven!

<u>Being a Bishop/Pastor/Preacher/Teacher/Deacon</u>, **DOES NOT** make you Christian or get you to Heaven!

Obtaining <u>religious college training/degrees</u>, **DOES NOT** make you a Christian or get you to Heaven!

Serving God, the way you think is right, **<u>DOES NOT</u>** make you a Christian or get you to Heaven!

Holding man/or <u>self-appointed church positions or titles</u>, **DOES NOT** make you a Christian or get you to Heaven!

Being <u>acknowledged by your Pastor</u> as a Christian, **<u>DOES NOT</u>** make you a Christian or get you to Heaven!

Being <u>in a false religion</u> that doesn't accept Jesus as the Son of God, **<u>WILL NOT</u>** get you to Heaven!

<u>Please take the time to meditate on the above things that do not make you a Christian and will not get you to Heaven!</u>

CHAPTER 10
MAYBE YOU WERE LEFT BEHIND BECAUSE YOU NEVER BEEN BORN-AGAIN!

WHAT THIS CHAPTER IS ABOUT
NOW THAT WE HAVE EXAMINED THINGS THAT DOESN'T MAKE YOU A CHRISTIAN IN THE PREVIOUS CHAPTER, I WISH NOW TO BE EVEN MORE STRAIGHTFORWARD IN SOME OF THE PRIMARY REASONS THAT YOU MAY HAVE BEEN LEFT BEHIND! OVER THE NEXT FEW CHAPTERS I WISH TO DELVE INTO SOME SPECIFICE AREAS IN WHICH THE ENEMY WAS DECEIVING CHURCH GOERS TO BELIEVE THEY WERE CHRISTIANS. IN THIS CHAPTER LETS LOOK AT SOME REAL POSSIBILITIES AROUND THE NOTION THAT YOU MAY HAVE NEVER BELONGED TO CHRIST!

(Romans 8:9) But ye are not in the flesh, but in the Spirit, if so be that the Spirit of God dwell in you. Now if any man has not the Spirit of Christ, he is none of His.

(1)
Never Belonged To Christ
CHRIST RETURNED FOR HIS TRUE CHURCH

(1 Corinthians 1:13) Is Christ divided? Was Paul crucified for you? Or were ye baptized in the name of Paul?

Denominationalized men and women put a lot of weight on their denominational affiliation and doctrines, which is UNBIBLICAL! There was only ONE CHRISTIAN CHURCH ON PLANET EARTH, and it was comprised of those who had repented of sin, were converted, and had experienced The Re-birth (or were Born-Again by the Spirit of God)! If you have not The SPIRIT OF CHRIST, you are none of His **(Romans 8:9)!** You can tell if you have Christ because you are changed, you are new:

(2Corinthians 5:17) Therefore if any man be in Christ, he is a new creature: old things are passed away; behold, all things are become new.

And if you have not been changed, you have not been saved! But if you have **The SPIRIT OF CHRIST,** you have been changed!

<u>So the question you should be asking yourself as a result of the statements I just made are</u>: Did you become a different or are you same sinful person you always were? Did your lifestyle change? Do you feel convicted if you commit sin?   Do you have a different mindset and direction?   And did all this take place after you confessed to be a Christian?

We are living in a time when people feel they can maintain sinful lifestyles and still confess Christianity! Well, it is not the character of a Christian to willfully continue in sin just because he/she thinks they have been set free from damnation by Jesus Christ!

> **(Romans 6:1, 2)** **What shall we say then? Shall we continue in sin, that grace may abound? God forbid. How shall we, that are dead to sin, live any longer therein?**

Those who were truly saved or truly **The Children of God** have been **Raptured** and are, at this moment, in Heaven with Jesus! They were in **The True Church** or as the Bible terms it: **THE BODY OF CHRIST** and have been translated to Glory to be with the Lord! **CHRIST CAME BACK ONLY AFTER HIS TRUE CHURCH, NOT THOSE WHO THOUGHT THEY WERE CONNECTED TO HIM!**

The Rapture is based upon **(1Thessalonians 4:16)** **that says: For the Lord Himself shall descend from Heaven with a shout, with the voice of the archangel, and with the trump of God: and the dead <u>in Christ</u> shall rise first:**

I know I have given you this knowledge in **Chapters 6 & 7 but** let me refresh your memory to reinforce what I am now saying! Let it be understood that it was Jesus Himself that came for His own! Before those living were gathered, all the Saints who slept (bodily physically dead) in Christ were gathered first!   So, during The Rapture, the first act was the gathering of the departed Saints; and next, the gathering of the living Saints. So you can see all those who were In-Christ and that have been Raptured are in Heaven shouting for joy! So, since you were not raptured, it means you were not in-Christ!

(John 14:2-3) *In my Father's house are many mansions: if it were not so, I would have told you. I go to prepare a place for you. And if I go and prepare a place for you, I will come again, and receive you unto myself; that where I am, there ye may be also.*

(2)
<u>Never Belonged To Christ</u>
<u>YOU MAY HAVE NEVER BEEN TRULY BORN-AGAIN!</u>

(John 3:3) Jesus answered and said unto him, Verily, verily, I say unto thee, Except a man be born again, he CANNOT SEE THE KINGDOM OF GOD.

I went into an in depth discussion on how to be born-again in Chapter 5, please re-read it! There is a possibility that you have not experienced **The Rebirth**, for without it **YOU CANNOT SEE OR ENTER INTO THE KINGDOM OF GOD!** The Holy Spirit is indicating to me that there are many that were deceived in this area, for anyone thinking that they could be saved under their own terms, is deceived by the enemy! Every person that is born-again had to conform to the Word and God and not God conform to them! For example, no one would blindly take a trip without looking at a map prior to the trip to investigate the correct route insuring they properly reach their destination! Neither will they blindly get on any highway and start driving in any direction! Why didn't you take the same precautions in your attempt to go to Heaven and truly know God?

Today there seems to be confusion as to what it means to be BORN-AGAIN! Being a Christian is not an intellectual reality for God cannot be known with your flesh (your mind). God is a SPIRIT, and they that worship HIM must worship HIM in spirit and in truth! Today, many know OF GOD but do not truly KNOW GOD! Knowing God means to have a heart to please God and a heart that is pleasing to God! **(John 14:15)** Without THE REBIRTH, one cannot SEE (comprehend) or ENTER INTO (access) THE KINGDOM OF GOD **(John 3:3,5)!** THE KINGDOM OF GOD is spiritual in nature and can only be entered by the spirit of man (THE INNER MAN) **(John 3:6)!** THE REBIRTH is the life and power of Jesus Christ operating within, which causes one to pursue right relationship with God that is based on faith!   The enemy, Satan, has erroneously converted the worship of God to an OUTWARD RITUAL, when in reality; a true relationship with God is an INNER REALITY, which is revealed outwardly! **TO TRULY BE BORN-AGAIN ONE MUST MAKE A SPIRITUAL TRANSACTION WITH** GOD! Please study Chapter 5 again for more clarity on this subject!

(3)
<u>Never Belonged To Christ</u>
<u>YOU MAY HAVE NOT UNDERSTOOD WHAT THE TRUE CHURCH WAS</u>

The Rapture has taken place, and the man-made Christian Church comprised of numerous divisional denominations have been left behind by Christ, is still divided; whereas the true Body of Christ, which was ONE, has been removed from the earth! Christ has come and hand-picked those in-Him out of the earth! Please understand that the true Christian Church was not an organization or a denomination.   The enemy came in through denominational organizations and sliced up Christian assemblies dividing them against each other! Did not Jesus say, united you stand and divided you fall, and a kingdom divided against itself cannot stand! If you were indoctrinated into the **denominational affiliation** mentality or man-made church organizations and did not realize that **The True Christian Church** was **ONE BODY MADE UP OF MANY MEMBERS**, you were side-tracked by Satan!   A tactic of the enemy is to DIVIDE & CONQUER! I am sure there were many professing Christianity who have been left behind because they did not know what the true Church was, therefore, they could not get into it! Please look at these scriptures.

> **_(1Corinthians 1:13)_   <u>Is Christ divided</u>? was Paul crucified for you? or were ye baptized in the name of Paul?**
> **_(Romans 12:5)_ So we, being many, are <u>ONE BODY in Christ</u>, and**

every one members one of another.
(<u>Ephesians 1:22</u>)   And hath put all things under his feet, and gave him to be the head over all things to <u>The Church,</u>
(<u>John 17:21</u>) That they all may be <u>ONE</u>; as thou, Father, art in Me, and I in Thee, THAT THEY ALSO MAY BE <u>ONE IN US</u>: that the world may believe that thou hast sent Me.

One of the greatest deceptions of the enemy may have been to cause you to believe that The Church is an organization, a building, your denomination, a place you go to!   Maybe you identified The Church with a material entity where you gathered to have an energetic ceremonial service rather than The Church being a **body of called out people that were all In-Christ!**   A body doesn't work against itself, it is not divided, but all parts work in synchronization and in union! The Church was **A LIVING ORGANISM**, not organizations comprised of many divisions (associations/affiliations)!   Those who were part of The Church were united with Christ and have been translated into Heavenly places because they were In-Christ who is the HEAD OF HIS BODY!

> *(<u>Colossians 1:12-13</u>) Giving thanks unto the Father, which hath made us meet to be partakers of the inheritance of the Saints in light: Who hath delivered us from the power of darkness, and hath translated us into the Kingdom of His dear Son:*

Because of that, God has omitted their sin, was open to their prayers, and adopted them into His family! Being IN-CHRIST, they had access and were made alive to God In-Him!   Man has erroneously made The Church into an organization built on divisions, powers and controls! The only Power is God and the only Controller is Jesus: blessed be to those who are spiritually united as one in Him!   I gave my allegiance to Jesus Christ, who is the Head of His Church, which is the MYSTICAL BODY OF CHRIST ON THE EARTH, can you say you truly did that?   This could be the reason you were left behind, because you did not truly understand what The True Church was, that it was not many, but it was ONE comprised of all people who were Born-Again regardless of affiliation or denomination and <u>Christ is the Head of It</u>!

(4)
<u>Never Belonged To Christ</u>
<u>MAYBE YOU WERE CAPTURED BY ANOTHER GOSPEL</u>

(Galatians 1:6) *I marvel that ye are so soon removed from him that called you into the grace of Christ unto another gospel:*

Now I added this here because I believe that there are those <u>who could have once been In-Christ</u> that <u>have been diverted from the Gospel of Truth</u>! And if that is you, it would be as if you have never belonged to Christ because you have forsaken the truth of His Word and been Left Behind!   It seems the Apostle Paul warns in the above scripture that there are some that have been removed from Christ because of the deception of another gospel! The Bible warned that in the End of Time another gospel would be preached that would **exclude** repentance from sin, the rebirth, the stressing of obedience, consecration, and separation from the world, the very foundations of The Doctrine of Christ!   This other gospel would not stress that there is only ONE WAY TO HEAVEN, and it is through JESUS CHRIST, but divert you to believe there are things that <u>you can do</u> to make you acceptable to God!   It was warned that in THE END false doctrine would be preached, practiced, & permitted originating from THE WORLD AND NOT CHRIST!   In these end times, the Bible warns also that there would be those who will not endure sound doctrine but would desire leaders that would tell them what they wanted to hear! And what is another gospel, the Bible says it is a gospel that would tickle their ears and make them laugh.   Meaning they wanted an unconvicting or feel good gospel that will ignore their sins!

(2Timothy 4:3- 4) *For the time will come when they will not endure sound doctrine; but after their own lusts shall they heap to themselves teachers, having itching ears; And they shall turn away their ears from the truth, and shall be turned unto fables.*

I saw it with my own eyes and as a Minister of Truth, for I

had many reject my messages and my ministry because I would not preach and teach another gospel to make them feel good! They wanted a gospel that doesn't put any demands on them, not demanding they separate from the world, repent, be consecrated, dedicated, or holy before God!   They did not want to hear the phrase 'personal sacrifice' it was completely out of the question! They loved Leaders that would overlook their sins as the phrase "DON'T JUDGE ME" advanced through the world and through the churches! They loved the false teaching that their tithes made them righteous without demanding that they had to live a life of righteousness to truly be righteous! The Bible warned that the false Leaders in the End Days would merchandised them, by teaching them the false doctrine of tithing or "GIVE TO GET" which is a doctrine not given to **the New Testament Church but extracted from the Old Testament Law and brought and served to the New Testament Church!**

> *(2Peter 2:3)   And through covetousness shall they with feigned words make merchandise of you: whose judgment now of a long time lingereth not, and their damnation slumbereth not.*

Those in the End of Time were made to believe that if they didn't pay **(tithes)** they would disintegrate into damnation, but that by paying them was an indication that they were righteous, and that it was the only way they could extract material or any type of blessing from God!

> *(Galatians 2:21)   I do not frustrate the Grace of God: for if righteousness come by The Law, then Christ is dead in vain.*

Because all individuals are held responsible that they obey the truth of God's Word, there is no excuse for being deceived when the warnings are in God's Word to **let no man deceive you (See Matthew 24:4; Mark 13:5; Ephesians 5:6; 2Thessalonians 2:3; and 1John 3:7)!** So, if you are following false leaders and their false doctrines and not the Word of God and were misguided, it could be the primary reason that Christ left you behind! Please read the following:

> *(Galatians 1:6-8) I marvel that ye are so soon removed from him that called you into the Grace of Christ unto ANOTHER GOSPEL*
> *(Galatians 1:9) As we said before, so say I now again, If any man preach any OTHER GOSPEL unto you than that ye have received, let him be accursed.*
> *(Galatians 2:21) I do not frustrate The Grace of God: for if righteousness come by The Law, then Christ is dead in vain.*
> *(Luke 8:12) Those by the way side are they that hear; then cometh the devil, and taketh away THE WORD out of their hearts, lest they should believe and be saved.!*
> *(2Peter 2:3) And through covetousness shall they with feigned words make merchandise of you: whose judgment now of a long time lingereth not, and their damnation slumbereth not.*
> *(Galatians 3:1-3) O foolish Galatians, who hath bewitched you, that ye should not obey the truth, before whose eyes Jesus Christ hath been evidently set forth, crucified among you? This only would I learn of you, Received ye the Spirit by the Works of The Law (OT), or by the hearing of faith (NT)? Are ye so foolish? having begun in the Spirit, are ye now made perfect by the flesh?*

The following questions are key signals for you to contemplate that there is a strong possibility that you were under the preaching and teaching of another gospel and were being taught things that were contrary or opposite of the truth of God's Word! Any of the following things could have been reasons you were LEFT BEHIND, so, let's examine and see if you recognize some of these **FALSE DOCTRINES & TEACHINGS**!

Did you listen to and believe **another gospel** message that was **not rooted in the Word of God for the New Testament Saints?**

Did the message you were taught **reject Grace through Faith** and magnify works such as **Tithing?**

Were you being taught that **God does not freely bless His Children** and that **one must pay God to bless them?** **(Old Testament Works of The Law).**

Did they know how to **Rightly Divide the Word of Truth,** or were your teachers **mixing The Works of the Law with Grace?**

Was **guilt put against those that did not contribute monetary funds** (Tithing)?

Was it alluded to or even taught outright that **righteousness is determined by your contributions to God**?

Did you feel **convicted of sin** or did your church leadership **avoid the subject of sin and sin issues**?

Did your church leadership **compromises righteousness and holiness** and simply ignored the truth of God's position on these subjects?

Are your **church leaders void of true spiritual knowledge and understanding** and were unable to delve into the deeper truths and things of God?

Are the people of your church made to feel guilty if they refuse to conform to the doctrine of monetary support of the church **(Tithing)?**

Does your church **allow worldly activities, entertainment and functions that are common in the world to infiltrate church services**?

Does **leadership accept homosexuals and lesbians into the ranks of the congregation**: what is their position on the activity or lifestyles of homosexuals are they open to it?

Is your church leadership in agreement with same-sex marriage which violates the sanctity of marriage as ordained by God?

And **do your church leaders attempt to deliver homosexuals** from the bondage of perversion by leading them to salvation through The Lord Jesus Christ?

Would you say your **church leaders are people pleasers or focused on pleasing God regardless of the consequences?**

Would you say your church leaders are more focused on the **Doctrines of Man or The Doctrine of Christ?**

Would you say your church leaders **do not preach or teach true salvation, repentance, the re-birth, and** holiness?

Would you say your church leaders are **focused more on materialism and money rather than saving of souls**?

Would you say your church **believes in commercializing, selling and merchandising in the Church**?

Is there **a price put on the Word of God and activities in your church** (fund raisers, banquets, tapes, videos, tickets, etc.)?

Is your church denominationally focused, primarily avoiding fellowship with assemblies which are not of your affiliation?!

So, the question you must ask yourself now is: could you have fallen by the wayside? It seems that people are shocked that I could indicate the possibility that they may have fallen away from God's Word, but it is not I that says it, it is **The Word of God**! Anyone that does not receive the seed of The Word, **CAN FALL BY THE WAYSIDE!** Without the truth of the Word of God, anyone can be deceived! In spiritual warfare it is a fact that The Devil will attempt to disengage The Word of God from taking root in your life! **Please do not fight against these communications, but just consider them, they could be a lifeline for your soul and the task that is at hand!**

(5)
Never Belonged To Christ
MAYBE YOU THOUGHT JUST SAYING YOU WERE A CHRISTIAN MADE YOU ONE

(Matthew 7:21) NOT EVERYONE THAT SAYS TO ME, Lord, Lord, shall enter into the Kingdom of Heaven; but he that does the will of my Father in Heaven.
(Luke 13:27) But He shall say, I tell you, I know you not whence ye are; depart from Me, all ye workers of iniquity.

JUST SAYING YOU ARE A CHRISTIAN DOESN'T MAKE YOU A CHRISTIAN! Today, there are individuals claiming to be Christians saying they believe in God, thinking just by saying they are Christians, makes them one, but being a Christian is more than just saying it!   If you were one of these individuals, it could be the primary reason you were left behind! Such an individual would be confused if asked to define what it means to be saved or what is True Christianity? I used to ask individuals who wanted to become a members of my Church Assembly to tell me and the church about their salvation and how God saved them. You would be surprised at the number of individuals who had no idea what I was talking about and did not understand what it meant to be Born-Again by the Spirit of God! Many in these End Times cannot give a confession of true salvation because Satan has subverted truth through false teachings of false preachers who themselves do not know what true salvation is and are teaching the people false doctrines!   They are causing people to believe that God is lenient to sin, and that God will overlook sinful lifestyles! Before you allow the enemy to upset you, read the Gospels and the Epistles and you will see that the focus of the Church was to lead people to Jesus Christ first and then baptize them, not just accept them as Christians! And not just baptizing them and telling them they are now Christians! In the End of Time, the view of what the true Church is, had become distorted! It is relevant to understand that one must submit to God and His Word! Many in these End Times can talk it but refuse to walk it! To confess Christianity without attempting to live a Christian life is ridiculous! If one truly believes in God (has faith) such a one will submit their life to God!   Many today, in these End Days, say they love Jesus but are living in total disobedience and rebellion against His spoken Word! Today, there are numerous individuals who believe that God must submit to them rather than they submit to God and that sinful and worldly activity is acceptable to a Holy and Righteous God! These individuals are deceitful in their activities; and avoid at all cost true dedication, worship and commitment to God and the Church!   Please make up your minds today to commit your life to the Living God, because **CONFESSION WITHOUT PROGRESSION** in the things of Christ may be the reason why you have been left behind!

(6)
<u>Never Belonged To Christ</u>
<u>BECAUSE YOU HAVE PLACED YOURSELF IN CHURCH</u>

POSITIONS, GOD DID NOT CALL YOU!

***(Matthew 7:22-23)** "Many will say to me in that day, Lord, Lord, have we not prophesied in thy name? and in thy name have cast out devils? and in thy name done many wonderful works? And then will I profess unto them, I never knew you: depart from me, ye that work iniquity.*

The Holy Spirit ordered me to add this to the book just before publishing. That there are many professing to be Christians in these End Days who have heaped upon themselves titles and positions within the Christian Church because titles of authority are attractive to them!   These are false leaders and false prophets! Despite all their professions, they are evil doers. Their religion expended itself in professions and prayers. Hence, in "that day" they are commanded to depart. What is meant for Jesus to say depart we may learnt from **(Matthew 25:41).**   It is evident from this passage that many are self-deceived.   No one can operate in the Body of Christ who is not placed or called by Christ who is the Head!   Men and women **ARE CALLING THEMSELVES** Apostles, Bishops, Pastors, Preachers, Teachers, Prophets, Minister, Elders, and an array of titles not even given in the Word of God, as they deceitfully operate amongst the New Testament Church! Many are lying saying "The Lord" called them when Jesus did not! These false individuals place themselves to mislead the people of God, seeking self-gratification, and positions which allow them to merchandise the flocks!   Many of them look at the Church as "a career" rather than a service or calling of God!   They are trained in the schools and universities of men rather than the School of the Holy Spirit!   They seek degrees in divinity rather than anointing from God to do His work!   They are liars and deceivers and do not understand that the Work of God is a spiritual work focus on a spiritual kingdom and the knowledge thereof must be imparted from God Himself upon those whom He chooses!   If you were involved in this mindset placing yourself in the church, it could be a reason you are left behind!

CHAPTER 11
MAYBE YOU WERE LEFT BEHIND
BECAUSE YOU LOVED SEX SINS!

WHAT THIS CHAPTER IS ABOUT
NOW THAT WE HAVE EXAMINED THE POSSIBILITY THAT YOU MAY HAVE NEVER
BEEN A CHRISTIAN IN THE PREVIOUS CHAPTER, I WISH NOW TO BE EVEN MORE
STRAIGHTFORWARD IN ONE OF THE PRIMARY REASONS THAT YOU MAY HAVE
BEEN LEFT BEHIND: SEX SINS! LETS LOOK INTENSELY AT THINGS THAT
WEREN'T BASED ON A LACK OF KNOWLEDGE BUT ON DECISIONS MADE ON
YOUR PART! IT IS UP TO THE INDIVIDUAL TO BE A SAINT OR SINNER, TO SEEK
TRUTH AND TO ENDURE TO KNOW THE TRUTH OF THE WORD OF GOD FOR
THEMSELVES! IN OTHER WORDS IT WAS UP TO YOU TO FOLLOW CHRIST AND
NOT MEN!   GOD GIVES US FREE WILL TO DECIDE WHOM WE WILL SERVE! LETS
LOOK AT SOME OF THESE THINGS!

---

(1)
Sex Sins Are An Abomination To God
YOU THOUGHT IT WAS OKAY TO CONTINUE IN SEX SIN

*(Romans 6:12) Let not sin therefore reign in your mortal body, that
ye should obey it in the lusts thereof.*

Any sinful activity is an abomination to God!   I am focused
on **SEX SINS** in this chapter because the world is so saturated
with it!   I want to point out to you the primary sexual acts that
humanity is involved in now that can damn your soul!   Satan who
is trying to take souls from God knows that one cannot confess
Christ, be unmarried under the guidelines of God's Word, and
continue to be willfully sexually active! He knows those active in
the numerous forbidden sex-related pursuits of mankind will cause
many to be damned with him in the Lake of Fire! **SEX SINS** are
a serious matter that can separate you from God and The Lord
Jesus Christ is not okay with anyone professing Christianity being
UNCLEAN! Recall in **John Chapter 8** the prostitute who was
caught in the very act of adultery, and when the false religious
leaders confronted Jesus about stoning her, Jesus reminded them
they also were sinners! After they dispersed, Jesus ministered to
her asking her where were her accusers?   Of course, Jesus forgave

her, but His final Word to her was – **"GO AND SIN NO MORE!"**

> *(John 8:11)   She said, No man, Lord. And Jesus said unto her, neither do I condemn thee: go, and sin no more.*

But a day is coming when Jesus will say to those who are false and have refused to follow Him and His Word regardless of what they confess:

> **(Matthew 7:22-23) Many will say to me in that day, Lord, Lord, have we not prophesied in thy name, cast out devils sand done many wonderful works? Then will I profess unto them, I NEVER KNEW YOU: DEPART FROM ME, YE THAT WORK INIQUITY!**

For Jesus to say, **I NEVER KNEW YOU** is another way of Him saying, **YOU NEVER KNEW HIM!**   Many professed to be Christians **THAT DID NOT KNOW JESUS**!   To know Jesus is to obey His will. **(See John 14:15; Matthew 7:21; 1 John 2:17)** Beware, **the continuous practice of iniquity** **(sin)** will obstruct a true relationship with Jesus Christ! **(Romans 6:15)** A profession of Christianity will not be enough, because if you were practicing iniquity, in this case SEX SINS, God classifies you as an evil doer! Satan, through his false prophets, broadcast the lie that one can continue in sin and have a true relationship with God!   But the Bible says in that day **(in the End of Time)** those who work iniquity are commanded to depart **(See Matthew 25:41)**!   This indicates that many are deceiving themselves to think that God is lenient to their continuous sinful sexual lifestyles! The true nature of sin is transgression, violating the divine boundary between good and evil **(See Psalms 51:1; Luke 15:29).**   Iniquity is departure from righteousness **(See Psalms 51:9; Romans 3:23)** & failure to meet the divine standard!   My appeal to you, even now in this dark hour, is to depart now from evil and - **HEAR YE THE WORD OF GOD & BE SAVED!!**   For through the finished work of Jesus Christ, if you truly accept Him, you can be given power to deny the prompts of the flesh! **LET NOT SIN THEREFORE REIGN**; be not its slave in being or doing wrong but be the freemen and willing servants of Christ in being and doing right. **IN YOUR MORTAL BODIES** meaning, let not your mind be enslaved to, or polluted by the bodily inclinations, appetites, or passions. Control and regulate them according to the will of God!!! **THIS IS YOUR FIGHT, AND THROUGH THE LORD JESUS CHRIST, YOU SHALL BE EMPOWERED, FOR**

GOD IS CALLING YOU TO DO THIS WORK!

(2)
<u>Sex Sins Are An Abomination To God</u>
<u>YOU WERE OPEN TO PERVERTED SEX SINS</u>

(<u>2 Corinthians 6:17</u>) calls for the Church to cleanse itself from pagan pollutions.
(<u>2Corinthians 6:17</u>) Wherefore come out from among them, and be ye separate, saith the Lord, and touch not the unclean thing; and I will receive you,

Homosexuality, lesbianism, sodomy, same sex marriages, lewdness (profanity, vulgarity), adultery, fornication, pornography, masturbation (self-gratification), oral sex, living out of wedlock, unclean imaginations, cross-dressing, bisexual, transgender, transsexual, intersex, a sexual, pansexual, etc. ---- all are common and accepted practices in the world and among many professing to be Christians in these LAST DAYS! Many in these END TIMES are practicing many of the evils mentioned above and more and are deceived to believe they are still children of God! Those who have been Left Behind should now know that you cannot participate in these things and still be accept by Jesus Christ as a Child of God! I don't care how much you went to church or how strong your testimony was! The Lord says His people are to come out from among them; in other words, if you are a Child of God you are not to do what those in the world are doing! Do not unite with them, or agree with them; it bothered me like Lot was vexed, but it vexed me that Christian churches in the End of Time were accepting the sin practices of the world rather than standing on God's Word! The Bible tells those that are godly that we should not encourage or connive at any of their idolatrous or wicked practices!

(<u>Acts 15:20</u>) But that we write unto them, that they abstain from pollutions of idols, and from fornication, and from things strangled, and from blood.
(<u>1Peter 1:14, 16</u>) As obedient children, not fashioning yourselves according to the former lusts in your ignorance: Because it is written, Be ye holy; for I am holy.

The Body of a Saint is God's temple and should have nothing

in common with the idol temple (sinners or temples of evil), so the saints are to be separated from the wicked and are to not accept their rebellious beliefs and practices! For ye are the temple of the living God!   The Christian is himself the sanctuary of the Lord, as is proved by the passage quoted from,

> **(<u>Leviticus 26:12</u>) And I will walk among you, and will be your God, and ye shall be my people.**

God dwells in His people as the Shekinah dwelt between the cherubim

> **(<u>Exodus 25:22</u>)   And there I will meet with thee, and I will commune with thee from above the mercy seat, from between the two cherubim which are upon the ark of the testimony, of all things which I will give thee in commandment unto the children of Israel. (<u>Isaiah 52:11</u>) Depart ye, depart ye, go ye out from thence, touch no unclean thing; go ye out of the midst of her; be ye clean, that bear the vessels of the LORD.**

(3)
<u>Sex Sins Are An Abomination To God</u>
<u>FORNICATION IS AN ABOMINATION AGAINST YOUR OWN BODY</u>

(<u>1Corinthians 6:9</u>) Know ye not that the unrighteous shall not inherit the kingdom of God? Be not deceived: neither <u>fornicators</u>, nor <u>idolaters</u>, nor adulterers, nor <u>effeminate</u>, nor abusers of themselves with mankind,

Fornication and adultery is illicit sexual intercourse outside the sanctity of marriage as ordained by God. This means marriage between a man and a woman. I want you to know that the Bible declares that neither **fornicators or adulterers shall inherit the Kingdom of God!** It is a fact that in the world **<u>fornication is rampant</u>** along with **<u>men and women living together outside the sanctity of marriage;</u>** both are committing illicit sex that is not ordained by God! If **<u>you are a fornicator or adulterer</u>**, it most definitely will be a reason for you to be Left Behind! The true Church (God's Kingdom on earth), and its faithful members, inherited **The Heavenly Kingdom (Matthew 25:34)**. So, those in **The Church, taken in the Rapture, obeyed the commandment of God regarding this issue!**

> **(<u>1Thessalonians 4:3</u>) For this is the will of God, even your sanctification (or holiness of life), that ye should abstain from fornication.**

Yes, I am **The Endtime Watchman;** I will deal with these

subjects, and I am speaking specifically to **PROFESSING CHRISTIANS,** not to those in the world for I expect those in the world to not obey God. **'Fornication' is sexual intercourse or having sexual relations outside the marital relationship** and what the world calls free love. Whereas **'Shacking' is a man and woman living together out of wedlock**! Living together outside of the sanctity of marriage is acceptable to the world but it is a transgression to GOD! Christians are to live righteous and obedient to the Will of God and if you violated the Word of God in this area it is one of the reasons you were Left Behind! Being a Pastor, I was aware that many professing Christians are living in these conditions and saw a lot of it among professing Christians! By the SPIRIT OF GOD, I never condoned it, but would tell the people to repent and submit to the Word of God! **God forbids fornication and shacking! I call for you to FORSAKE COMMITTING FORNICATION because Christ will not accept you into His Kingdom unless you repent, turn away from its sinful activity and obey Him!**

> ***(1 Corinthians 6:18)** Flee fornication. Every sin that a man does is without the body; but he that commits fornication sins against his own body.*

The reason this is such an abomination is because fornication and adultery creates a 'unholy union' during sexual relations, resulting in **Spiritual ONENESS!**

> In ***(1 Corinthians 6:15-16)** Know ye not that your bodies are the members of Christ? Shall I then take the members of Christ, and unite them with the members of a harlot? God forbid! What? Know ye not that he which is joined to a harlot is one body? For the two shall be one flesh.*

If you wish to profess Christianity, you should abstain from fornication & adultery because it is a sin **AGAINST YOURSELF!** If you wish to be IN-CHRIST, spiritually and become one spirit with Him, allow **YOUR BODY** to become **THE TEMPLE OF GOD; recognize the sacredness of that!** The guilt of sin associated with fornication and adultery and the spiritual and physical consequences can cause damnation to the soul! **(Read Galatians 5:19-21)**

(4)
<u>Sex Sins Are An Abomination To God</u>
<u>**HOMOSEXUALITY IS A SATANIC ENTICEMENT**</u>

(Romans 1:24) Wherefore God also gave them up to uncleanness through the lusts of their own hearts, to dishonor their own bodies between themselves:

Because I am The Endtime Watchman and because I am sent to Release Spiritual Knowledge, I must say something on this subject because I hate the wiles of the devil!

To those who are **effeminate (male homosexuals)** and **lesbians (female homosexuals),** unless you repent and accept Jesus Christ as Lord, you shall not inherit the **Kingdom of God** and shall have your part in the **Lake of Fire!** Homosexuality is a shameful act quite prevalent among the heathen. The first submitting themselves to foul sensuality, and the second actively abusing themselves with mankind, both contrary to nature! Both are termed as Sodomites, perverted in nature! I listed in this chapter in section **(2)** <u>**YOU WERE OPEN TO SEX SINS AND PERVERSIONS**</u> None who are guilty of any one of the lists of vices given can be an **Heir of Heaven.** Be not deceived. Let no one make the mistake of thinking that any unrighteous individual shall be an Heir. If one participates in these things, such a one(s) will not see Heaven's Gates!

The reason I speak strongly regarding homosexuality is because in these End Days I recognized how the enemy, Satan, has extensively promoted this activity, and I war against the enemy! Homosexuality (and as noted this term refers to male and females because a lesbian is a female homosexual) is an abomination in the eyesight of God.

> ***(Romans Ro 1:24) Wherefore God also gave them up to uncleanness through the lusts of their own hearts, to dishonor their own bodies between themselves: (Please read also Romans 1:25-32)***
> ***(1 Corinthians 6:9) Know ye not that the unrighteous shall not inherit the kingdom of God? Be not deceived: neither fornicators, nor idolaters, nor adulterers, nor effeminate, nor abusers of themselves with mankind,***

God does not hate the homosexual or lesbian, but God hates the act of homosexuality! In **The Release of Spiritual Knowledge,** please allow me to impart to you how individuals are captured into this perverted lifestyle: Homosexuality is a satanic-induced rebellion, initiated by a demon spirit (perverse spirit), to nullify the institution of marriage between a man and a woman as ordained by God (destroying the family structure). The individual is captured into the lifestyle by enticement (seducing spirit) which leads to spiritual bondage (perverse spirit)! I wish to add for you to know how a person is enticed into this lifestyle: these demon spirits usually have opportunity because of **some type of experienced trauma**! Whether it be child molestation, abuse, or some type of injury to **the spirit of the individual** that causes a 'wound' or opening, allowing these demons to enter, operate and capture the individual. All spiritual bondage is obtained by **the submission of the will so when an individual's will is compromised or violated, the individual becomes accessible to evil spirits!**

> **(Leviticus 18:22) Thou shalt not lie with mankind, as with womankind: it is abomination.**

What exactly does God say about homosexuality is shown in the above scripture!   My focus is to **Release Spiritual Knowledge** so you can know the truth and I pray that you understand that **WHAT YOU BELIEVE** will determine your future eternal destination! Abominations are things/activities that **ARE NOT ACCEPTABLE TO THE LORD GOD** and I hope you see after progressing this far in the book that Satan and his forces of evil have perpetrated numerous deceptions in the minds of humanity!   I say again, be not deceived, no matter what is said, those practicing homosexuality and lesbianism shall not inherit the Kingdom of God!! Satan has caused "even professing Christians" to accept numerous abominations but understand that **SIN IS NOT CONSIDERED TO BE SIN TO THOSE WHO DO NOT KNOW CHRIST** because they have not truly accepted salvation through Jesus Christ, and cannot comprehend the things of God, so they are damned without Christ! I encourage you to meditate in **The Word of God** to transform your mind to hear God's voice only, not the world's! What does God say on this subject? **(Study the following scriptures)**

> **(Leviticus 20:13)   If a man also lie with mankind, as he lieth with a woman, both of them have committed an abomination: they shall surely be put to death; their blood shall be upon them.**
> **(Genesis 19:5)   And they called unto Lot, and said unto him, Where are the men which came in to thee this night? bring them out unto us, that we may know them.**
> **(Judges 19:22-24) Now as they were making their hearts merry, behold, the men of the city, certain sons of Belial, beset the house**

round about, and beat at the door, and spake to the master of the house, the old man, saying, Bring forth the man that came into thine house, that we may know him. And the man, the master of the house, went out unto them, and said unto them, Nay, my brethren, nay, I pray you, do not so wickedly; seeing that this man is come into mine house, do not this folly. Behold, here is my daughter a maiden, and his concubine; them I will bring out now, and humble ye them, and do with them what seemeth good unto you: but unto this man do not so vile a thing.

(1 Kings 14:24) And there were also sodomites in the land: and they did according to all the abominations of the nations which the LORD cast out before the children of Israel

(Romans 1:26-27) For this cause God gave them up unto vile affections: for even their women did change the natural use into that which is against nature: And likewise also the men, leaving the natural use of the woman, burned in their lust one toward another; men with men working that which is unseemly, and receiving in themselves that recompence of their error which was meet.

(1 Corinthians 6:9) Know ye not that the unrighteous shall not inherit the kingdom of God? Be not deceived: neither fornicators, nor idolaters, nor adulterers, nor effeminate, nor abusers of themselves with mankind,

(1 Timothy 1:10) For whoremongers, for them that defile themselves with mankind, for menstealers, for liars, for perjured persons, and if there be any other thing that is contrary to sound doctrine;

(Jude 1:7) Even as Sodom and Gomorrah, and the cities about them in like manner, giving themselves over to fornication, and going after strange flesh, are set forth for an example, suffering the vengeance of eternal fire.

Do not be deceived! Anyone practicing homosexuality and claiming to be a Christian is a liar and will be Left Behind! As God says in **(Jeremiah 7:10)**, how can you call yourself His child and are doing abominations in His sight, because His children do not have a desire to willfully continue in sin! Those still practicing homosexuality are not truly Children of God, for the true Children of God are new creatures, old things have passed away, behold all things are become new, that's why the true Children of God were taken in the Rapture!!! Children of God are **converted** from their old sinful lifestyles and given an inner desire to please God

(2Corinthians 5:17)!   So, beware, do not allow the **voice of the satanic world** to deceive you and alter your way of thinking by denying what God says about this!!   So, I hope we are clear on this subject: That homosexuality is a sin in the eyesight of God and anyone practicing it will not inherit the Kingdom of God!   Understand that God is Holy, and He hates all sin! The problem in the End Days is that people are listening to the satanic world and not to the Living God **(READ ROMANS 1:16-32**)!   God is not against the individual, for He loves all and wishes all to be converted from sin through the Lord Jesus Christ, but God is against sin and **HOMOSEXUALITY IS A SIN,** regardless of what the world says! God calls all those accepting Jesus Christ to repentance and progression in righteousness, He is not tolerant to the continuance of sin! If you or anyone embraces what the world teaches regarding the homosexuality lifestyle rather than truth of God's Word, you and others are in great error!   Homosexuality is designed to attack the foundation of God's will for the family and stability of humanity. I call for anyone who is a homosexual to repent and turn to Jesus for salvation today!

(5)
<u>Sex Sins Are An Abomination To God</u>
<u>SAME-SEX MARRIAGE – A VILE AND SINFUL ACT!</u>

<u>(Romans 1:26-27)</u> God gave them up to vile affections: their women changed to that which is against nature: & the men, leaving the woman, burned in their lust one toward another; men with men working that which is unseemly!

In concluding this chapter on **Sex Sins,** I wish to impart some knowledge on what has transpired recently before The Rapture of the Church occurred – **SAME SEX MARRIAGES!** God sanctioned the MARRIAGE relationship to be **<u>ONLY BETWEEN A MAN AND A WOMAN!</u>**   The Satanic System on the other hand, campaigning in opposition to the Will of God, has created same sex marriage in rebellion against the order of God!   I was shocked by those professing to be Christians who compromised the Word of God and submitted to the Satanic

System in accepting this perversion!   The focus of Satan is the destruction of the **family** and the obliteration of **humanity** by the cessation of proliferation of the races and desecration of the soul through homosexuality/lesbianism and sodomy!   The nations have degenerated to a level that illustrates the satanic influence over this evil world, his increasing overthrow of morality, and his success in converting the mindset of humanity from God to evil.   Jesus and prophets said that those things would be at the End of Time!   The fact that these things, along with other wiles Satan is seen to be working, illustrates that the **END OF TIME IS HERE! WILL YOU BELIEVE GOD OR SATAN?   THE CHOICE IS NOW YOURS!**

CHAPTER 12
MAYBE YOU WERE LEFT BEHIND
BECAUSE YOU EMBRACED FALSE WORSHIP

WHAT THIS CHAPTER IS ABOUT
NOW THAT WE HAVE EXAMINED IN THE PREVIOUS CHAPTER THE ABOMINATION OF SEX SINS. IN THIS CHAPTER I WISH TO LOOK AT HOW MANY PROFESSING CHRISTIANITY IN THE END TO TIME HAVE EMBRACED THE MINDSET OF THE WORLD AND HAVE ALLOWED THE INFILTRATION OF FALSE WORSHIP AND IDOLOTRY TO ENTER THE HOUSES OF PRAYER! IT IS MY DUTY TO GOD TO BE STRAIGHTFORWARD IN SOME OF THE PRIMARY REASONS THAT CHRIST TOOK THOSE WHO WERE A PART OF HIS CHURCH AND NOT YOU! LET'S LOOK INTENSELY AT FALSE WORSHIP IN THIS CHAPTER FOR IT MAY BE THE CAUSE YOU WERE LEFT BEHIND!

---

(1)
FALSE WORSHIP - UNACCEPTABLE TO GOD
DID YOU PARTICIPATED IN FALSE WORSHIP

(Galatians 2:4) And that because of false brethren unawares brought in, who came in privily to spy out our liberty which we have in Christ Jesus, that they might bring us into bondage.

Many things were being done in the End Time Churches that were not acceptable to God! The question I present is what was your position regarding those things? Were you open to allow the world in the church or were you opposed in your spirit to the world in the church! Maybe you could not do anything about how your church services were conducted, but God examines the heart assessing how you felt about these activities! In your heart, did you oppose worldliness in the church, or did you embrace it; that is what The Lord judges! For example, I was a Pastor and would not allow any crossover Christian music in my church! I didn't allow pantomime or ballet dancers, I ran my devotions the old-time way, and I did not condone homosexuality or allow homosexuals in the pulpit! If I discerned someone was homosexual, they knew my position on the matter and I sought to lead him/her to repent and be delivered and saved by the power of Jesus Christ! I didn't just baptize people and put their name on the church membership roll, but I made sure they understood how to accept Christ and make that commitment before they became members of the church I ran!   So, the question is, who did you stand with on the activities going on in your church? Did you stand on the righteousness of God or did you align yourself with those things which are false that invaded the Christian Church in this, **THE END OF TIME?**

(2)
FALSE WORSHIP - UNACCEPTABLE TO GOD
PANTOMIME (MIME)!

(Luke 1:64) And his mouth was opened immediately, and his tongue loosed, and he spake, and praised God.

One of the most shameful things I witnessed in the End Time Church was the infiltration of worldly entertainment into the worship services!   It was disturbing to me how 'church members' absorb themselves in the false worship!   The false leaders are going to be held responsible for what they allowed in the Houses of Prayer!   The Lord God knows whether you were receptive or should I say responsive to this fake form of worship!   Pantomime had no place in the Christian Church, praise and worship is A SOUND, --- NOT SILENCE!   I am sure that Satan was loving how he shut **the mouth of the church** with this form of fake, false, and mockery way of worshipping God!   Every interaction with God must be voiced! (prayer, confession, repentance, etc.).   But a mime artist (from the Greek, μῖμος, mimos, IMITATOR, ACTOR) is someone who uses a theatrical medium, acting out a story through bodily motions WITHOUT THE USE OF SPEECH!   Another term for this activity is to mummer. The word pantomime means ALL IMITATION which, in turn, means FALSE!   Acting or mimicking worship or praise is an abomination to God because Praise & Worship should originate from the spirit of God's people!

(3)
FALSE WORSHIP - UNACCEPTABLE TO GOD
A FORM OF GODLINESS!

(2Timothy 3:5)   Having A FORM OF GODLINESS, but denying the power thereof: from such turn away.

A FORM OF GODLINESS are people pretending to be Christians that do not perceive what true Christianity is, therefore they accept any and everything that makes them look like good

101

people! That means they will allow anything to come into the churches and will accept anything as allowable because they do not know or submit themselves to God!   They are open to worldly activities such as: Christian comedians, ballet dancers; all the different types of worldly music now designated as Christian (such as Christian rock, Christian rap, Christian rock, Christian blues, and Christian metal, homosexuals and lesbians and same sex marriage; all types of perversion and sex sins such as fornication, and adultery! They are false Christians having A FORM OF GODLINESS so out of wedlock living, celebration of pagan holidays, sin acceptance, and compromising The Word of God for gain are all things they are open to because they do not know God nor have been born-again of His Spirit! Other things the End Time church disintegrated into that haven't been mentioned were denominational divisions, worldly dress, women in authority over men, no real reverence for God or His Word, world mixing, and a refusal to submit to God's Will over what they desired to do! HAVING A FORM OF GODLINESS externally, but inwardly, were not of God, which is the primary reason many who were open and receptive to these activities and beliefs were LEFT BEHIND IN THE RAPTURE!   Before I end this paragraph, I must say something about those who, in the end of time, did not trust God's Word to convert them, for they were: **DENYING THE POWER;** illustrating by their lives that they did not have THE TRUE SPIRIT OF CHRIST and had not experienced its renewing and sanctifying power! But their religion was only A FORM OF GODLINESS; not real Christianity but an outward form or image!

(4)
FALSE WORSHIP - UNACCEPTABLE TO GOD
DID YOU THINK PAYING YOUR TITHES MADE YOU RIGHT WITH GOD?

(2 Corinthians 9:7) Every man according as he purposes in his heart, so let him give; not grudgingly, or of necessity: for God loves a cheerful giver.

The topic of Tithing disrupted the foundation of The Christian Church in this, THE END OF TIME! Many were led astray because of this Satanic lie! If you were a professing Christian, look around you, many that believed in this doctrine have been **LEFT BEHIND!**   GOD told me to dismantle that which is false and bring those being deceived back to the **TRUTH OF HIS WORD,** but many would not listen! Many thought the doctrine was in error but believed the false leaders over the Word of God!   Let's talk about the Old Testament Doctrine of Tithing! First understand that we were in The Dispensation of Grace; it is erroneous to teach Tithes (which were works of the law in the Old Testament) instead of **GRACE (**Unmerited Favor, as founded in the New Testament) **(READ 1 Timothy 2:15)!**   In the Old Testament Tithing was given to Israel to support the Levi Tribe (who were the Priest) because they were not allocated any land, they were keepers of the temple!   Everything a Christian **RECEIVES FROM GOD BEING HEIRS OF SALVATION** is freely given because of the work of Jesus Christ! God asks Christians, under the New Testament to Just Believe! **(Read Galatians 2:16-19; 3:22-24)** Because no man has been able to fulfill the Law, Satan has instigated the work of tithes converting Christians from **FAITH IN CHRIST** to **WORKS OF THE LAW** for he knows that those taking part in this doctrine will cause those who embrace it, and many did, to be judged under the Law by their works! **(Read Galatians 3:10; James 2:10; Revelation. 20:12-13)** It was easy for Satan to propagate the False Leaders in the false doctrine because they sought to merchandise the Saints!

> *(John 2:16) And said unto them that sold doves, Take these things hence; make not my Father's house an house of merchandise.*
> *(2Peter 2:3) And through covetousness shall they with feigned words make merchandise of you: whose judgment now of a long time lingereth not, and their damnation slumbereth not.*

Please listen carefully, I am sure God does not care how much you donate or give to the church for He loves a cheerful giver! The danger with the doctrine of tithing to the New Testament Church is when tithing replaces Grace in the hearts of those that give!   That is what was happening in these End Days!   Tithers seem to remove the work of Jesus Christ and replace Grace with 'their works' of paying God to bless them and consider them as being righteous before Him!   This is error, for we are saved by Grace through faith alone as rendered through the Lord Jesus Christ; it is a gift of God! No work of yourself can bless you or save you, it is strictly the work of Christ! But the enemy has diverted many from faith to works!

> **(Ephesians 2:8)**   **For by grace are ye saved through faith; and that not of yourselves: it is the gift of God:**

Another danger of the tithes doctrine is the Bible says in simple words that to be saved from the wrath of God, one must accept salvation only through the Lord Jesus Christ as our redeemer not our own works of righteousness! It goes on to say that anyone trying to establish their own righteousness, especially by works of the Law (tithing is a work of the Law) that individual will be judged by God by THE LAW! So, it is saying if such an individual has broken just one of the Ten Commandments (The Law) they are damned! That is why Jesus came to fulfill The Law! So I hope you can see the deception of the enemy (Satan) who has led many back into "a work of the Law" knowing that just one (1) sin will damn their soul if they remove their faith in Jesus Christ by attempting to be right with God under their own strength and efforts! **(Ephesians 2:8)**   Here are other scriptures!

> **(1John 3:4)** **"Whosoever committeth sin transgresseth also the law: for sin is the transgression of the law.**
> **(Philippians 3:9)** **And be found in him, not having mine own righteousness, which is of the law, but that which is through the faith of Christ, the righteousness which is of God by faith:**
> **(Romans 2:12)** **For as many as have sinned without law shall also perish without law: and as many as have sinned in the law shall be judged by the law;**

There are those that have lived on this earth that didn't have the Ten (10) Commandments and God will not judge them by the guidelines of The Law! An example of this is Abraham, his belief and obedience were counted unto him as righteousness because The Law had not been given! As many as have sinned under The Law., under a revelation of God's will, these shall be judged by it and condemned for disobedience to its commands. Now to put oneself back under The Law by going back under its guidelines of "works" means to put oneself back under being judge by it and no man has been able to keep it!

Through Christ Jesus, we have access to God and all that we are is in Christ Jesus, all is by Grace, not of works less any man should boast; it is a gift of God!   And by the way, **WE ARE ALREADY BLESSED; WE ARE CHILDREN OF GOD, HEIRS OF SALVATION, and ALL THINGS ARE OURS!**

So, what is the **NEW TESTAMENT** doctrine to the Saints for supporting ministry??? ------ **GIVING!!! --- NOT TITHING!** **(Study: 2 CORINTHIANS CHAPTERS 8 & 9; Luke 6:38; and Acts 20:35)**

CHAPTER 13
MAYBE YOU WERE LEFT BEHIND
YOU WERE INTO PAGAN RELIGION!

WHAT THIS CHAPTER IS ABOUT
IN THE PREVIOUS CHAPTER 12 I DEALT WITH FALSE WORSHIP WHICH AN
ABOMINATION IN THE EYESIGHT OF GOD.   I WISH TO TAKE YOU INTO AN
EXAMINATION OF PAGAN PRACTICES AND FALSE RELIGIONS THAT DO NOT
RECOGNIZE CHRIST THE ITS TRUE LORD AND IF THEY DO THEY HAVE
DISTORTED CHIRSTIANITY AND MIXED IT WHITH PAGANISM.   LET'S LOOK AT
SOME OF THESE THINGS!

(A)   PAGAN HOLIDAYS

Everyone professing to be Christians should be weary of pagan
holidays and avoid them for they are of pagan origin, unbiblical and
are not of God.   Christians should know the history and origin of
every holiday the world embraces for I guarantee you, they are not
of God.

(1)
PAGAN WORSHIP IS AN ABOMINATION TO GOD
MAYBE YOU WERE INVOLVED IN PAGAN WORSHIP AND
OBSERVANCES

I am The EndTime Watchman, I was sent to warn the people
of God of soul damning practices of the heathen and the
deceptions of Satan! Paganism is the exercise of <u>any religious
belief or practice other than Christianity</u>! Understand that there
are religions out there that claim to be Christian BUT ARE NOT!
In other words, any religion that is not centered on Jesus Christ, the
Son of the true and living God, is a false religion!   Paganism
worship and observances are a collection of religious movements
being revived or reconstructed from the historical Pre-Abrahamic
religions. There are roughly 300 million pagans worldwide! Satan
infiltrated the Christian faith with pagan practices and convinced
many who professed Christianity that these activities are harmless!
I always preached, that anything that **THE WORLD** embraces,
YOU SHOULD BE CAUTIOUS OF! Why….? because The
World is at enmity against God and the things of God!   By the

power of God, here are a few of the major pagan practices that Christians are embracing in these last days: Christmas, Christmas Trees, Mistletoe, Santa Claus, Halloween, Easter, Easter Eggs, Easter Bunny, Sunrise Services, Worship of Mary, Astronomy, Occultism, Tattoos, Piercings, Sexual Immorality, etc., etc.   I could go on and on!   I warned when I blew the trumpet on earth before **The Rapture** and now, I am warning you again, THESE ANCIENT RELIGIOUS PAGAN PRACTICES ARE TIED TO THE SATANIC WORSHIP OF DEMON ENTITIES AND ARE AN ABOMINATION TO THE LORD GOD!

(Revelation 18:4) And I heard another voice from Heaven, saying, come out of her, my people, that ye be not partakers of her sins, and that ye receive not of her plagues.
(James 4:4) Ye adulterers and adulteresses, know ye not that the friendship of the world is enmity with God? whosoever therefore will be a friend of the world is the enemy of God.

Do you celebrate CHRISTMAS? It is a PAGAN HOLIDAY! Any holiday celebrated in the Satanic world system that has symbols associated with it as you see Christmas: for example, Christmas Trees, Mistletoe, Santa Claus, etc. Jesus Christ WAS NOT born on December 25th!!! Also, the Xmas Tree is a pagan symbol!   So where did Xmas come from? Xmas is the celebration of the Roman Winter Solstice. It is the time at which the sun appears at noon at its lowest altitude above the horizon! In ancient times this day was associated with the worship of the SUN GODDESS! The Christmas tree is of pagan tradition/ritual surrounding the Winter Solstice, which included the use of many symbols, including tree worship! The celebration of Jesus's birthday along, with the pagan symbols associated with it, ARE NOT BIBLICAL AND ARE AN ABOMINATION TO GOD! God revealed HOW JESUS WAS BORN to illustrate His virgin birth and the fulfillment of prophecy which were KEYS marking the Plan of Redemption!

(Jeremiah 10:3-4) For the customs of the peoples are vanity; for one cut a tree out of the forest, the work of the hands of the workman with the axe. They deck it with silver and with gold; they fasten it with nails and with hammers, that it not move.

Easter is also a pagan holiday with its Easter Eggs, Easter Bunny, Sunrise Services along with Halloween which is a pagan holiday worshiping demons with its activities of

Trick-or-treat, pumpkins, evil costumes, jack-o-lantern, and apple-bobbing! I could go into the details of these evil festivities but that is not my purpose in this book, I wish only to inform you of how the enemy has deceived people to believe and accept things that were an abomination to God! But I must say something on the rampant advancement of tattooing, piercings or cutting of the flesh that surfaced in the End of the Age! For the Bible says about the following pagan practices:

(Leviticus 19:28) **'You shall not make any cuts in your body for the dead nor make any tattoo marks on yourselves: I am the LORD.**

Yes, that is right! Cutting the flesh (tatoos) is biblically associated with the worship of demons and mourning for the dead! These flesh scrapings progress communications with evil spirits and the symbols are associated with memorials, sorcery, enchantments, and encrypted (coded) data, which allow right of entry for evil entities! We are in the End of Time and the enemy has advanced this evil to prepare the masses for the reception of the **MARK OF BEAST** which shall doom the souls of individuals to the Lake of Fire! A watchword I used in my church is: **IF THE WORLD LOVES IT, ACCEPTS IT, AND ENGAGES IN IT, IT'S NOT OF GOD!**

(2)
<u>FALSE RELIGIONS ARE AN ABOMINATION TO GOD
NEW AGE DOCTRINE AND THINKING IS RAMPANT IN
THESE END TIMES</u>

The New Age doctrine and thinking is rampant in these end days and has deceived many! I am saying something specifically about it because it is a primary false teaching that Satan is projecting in this end age and many have attached themselves to this way of thinking.   Self is the main theme and focus; everyone is self-serving and self-motivated. This false teaching denies the idea of only one way to Heaven, so it denies what Jesus said when He said He is the way, the truth, and the life and no can come to the Father except through Him! You have heard many famous individuals say that they believe there are many ways to God so all religions are acceptable, this is a lie from Hell! This doctrine embraces most non-Christian theologies saying that there are many ways to Heaven.   It embraces the idea of evolution of both the body and the spirit and that reincarnation can be a part of that. It includes visualization and astral projection. It looks upon man as being good and divine (gods).   It teaches that each person can travel their own path as they understand it and that man is to have peace with and be in harmony with god, his fellow man and with creation. This doctrine teaches that a world leader will come to show them the way. Yes, I am sure you can see that this is the way many in the world think in these End Days which caused many to be left behind in The Rapture!!

B) <u>FALSE RELIGIONS ARE AN ABOMINATION TO GOD</u>
<u>MAYBE YOU WERE IN THE ROMAN CATHOLIC CHURCH - A FALSE RELIGION!</u>

(1Timothy 4:3) Forbidding to marry, and commanding to abstain from meats, which God hath created to be received with thanksgiving of them which believe and know the truth.

As you all should know, I stand not against any TRUE CHRISTIAN, regardless of denominational affiliation, but I am against man-made denominational structures which promote divisions and teach false doctrines! I have promised God to speak truth amid deception! And the truth is: The Roman Catholic Church (RCC) is the greatest pagan religion one the face of planet earth that will cause millions to lose their souls!   This denomination has led many astray and is leading many towards damnation! Many doctrines within this denomination are men's doctrines which conflict with the Word of God! For example: **FORBIDDING TO MARRY**: The RCC forbids the clergy, and induces monks and nuns to take vows of celibacy, declaring, that, whosoever shall say that the married state is to be preferred to a state of virginity or celibacy, let him be accursed. **ABSTAINING FROM MEATS:** Commanding to abstain from meats, which the RCC does during Lent, on fast-days, and days of abstinence. As the above scripture shows, these are just two (2) of the things the RCC teaches its membership that are against God's commandments! The Bible says in **(Hosea 4:6),** My people are destroyed for a lack of knowledge! WAKE UP AND HEAR THE WORD OF THE LORD! I could extend this section on the Roman Catholic Church and its deceptions but I must attempt to simply summarize it's evil activities:

<u>(1)</u>
<u>CALLING THE POPE AND PRIEST FATHER IN THE ROMAN CATHOLIC CHURCH</u>

***(Matthew 23:9)** And call no man your father upon the earth: for one is your Father, which is in Heaven.*

As Christians, we should always seek truth, we should never follow anything blindly! **(See Matthew 15:14)** Your Spiritual Father is God and Him only!!! The Roman Catholic Church was formed when the pagan religions of Rome merged with Christianity! Conditions in the Roman Empire facilitated the spread of new ideas. Unlike most religions in the Roman Empire, however, Christianity required its adherents to renounce all other gods, for God forbids idolatry. Before the formation of the Roman Catholic Church, Roman Christians refused to join pagan celebrations in the Roman Empire, which meant they were unable to participate in much of public life, which caused non-Christians to fear that the Christians were angering the gods and thereby threatening the peace and prosperity of the Empire. Roman Emperor Constantine I, in 313, legalized Christianity, and in 380 the Edict of Thessalonica made THE ROMAN CATHOLIC CHURCH the state church of the Roman Empire. With that legalization, pagan religions, along with their practices and rituals were merged into the Roman Catholic Church. That also brought along the infiltration of numerous pagan holidays, observances, practices, and symbols which represent the worship of pagan gods associated with the false religions of the Roman Empire and the demonic deities associated with them!!!

(2)
<u>FALSE RELIGIONS ARE AN ABOMINATION TO GOD SOME UNHOLY RITUALS OF THE ROMAN CATHOLIC CHURCH!</u>

***(Matthew 27:51)**   And, behold, the veil of the temple was rent in twain from the top to the bottom; and the earth did quake, and the rocks rent.*

Although I could go on and on, today, let's examine six (6) of the major rituals implemented in Catholicism that are **NOT BIBLICAL**!

1) AN EARTHLY PRIESTHOOD: The Pope decided to reserve the title of priest for its leaders in the Catholic Church! Along with the priesthood designation, the people are made liable to **CONFESS THEIR SINS TO THE PRIEST and not to God!** The earthly priesthood ended with the crucifixion of Jesus Christ, for the veil in the temple was torn rent from top to bottom and the holy of holies was open! The intercessor now between God and man is Jesus Christ the Lord! **(See Hebrews 2:17; 4:14-15; 8:1)**

2) THE USE OF BEADS, PRAYING REPETITVE PRAYERS: From pagan religions, the Roman Catholics initiated the praying with beads ritual! (For example: Hindus, Islam, Buddhist use beads to pray). Jesus speaks explicitly against repetitive prayers stating that it is a heathen practice! **(See Matthew 6:5-7).**

3) WORSHIP OF THE VIRGIN MARY: Roman Catholics heap 10 times more praise upon Mary than God Himself. Of the 59 total beads of the rosary, **(Romans sary ritual),** 53 beads are **Hail Mary's,** but only 6 beads are **Our Father.** The Rosary most often ends with a **Hail, Holy Queen** prayer to Mary, not God! The worship of Mary is the worship of the pagan, **Queen of Heaven! (Babylonian Goddess Ishtar)** which is an abomination to God!

4) BOWING DOWN TO GRAVEN IMAGES: Catholics bow down to idols, icons and images of Jesus, Mary, saints and the apostles, kissing the feet of the statues and praying to them. If you read the Catholic Bible you will see that the Pope deleted the 2nd of the 10 commandments so they could use statues & images in worship to satisfy the merger of paganism! The 10th commandment on coveting was split to still maintain ten (10) commandments in number. The Bible condemns creating or bowing to any graven image! **(Also see Exodus 20:4)**

> *(Leviticus 26:1)* **Ye shall make you no idols nor graven image, neither rear you up a standing image, neither shall ye set up any image of stone in your land, to bow down unto it: for I am the LORD your God.**

5) BAPTISM BY SPRINKLING: The Catholic church baptizes babies by sprinkling of water to signify this act makes

them a Christian! The Bible states to be saved one must first repent and believe, can babies do this? **(See Mark 16:16; Acts 8:36-37; Acts 2:38)**   In 1311 AD, the Catholic Council of Ravenna, declared that sprinkling was an acceptable substitute for immersion, thus, sprinkling replaced immersion in the Roman Catholic Church. The Bible teaches **total immersion** for baptism. **(See Matthew 3:16; Acts 8:38-39)**
6) INVENTION OF PAGAN HOLIDAYS: The Roman Catholic church has invented numerous non-biblical holy days like **Lent, Easter, and Christmas!** Due to space restraints, I have addressed only one, **CHRISTMAS! (Christ + Mass)** was first used in 1038 AD. Before 335 A.D., the pagan cult of Mithra, the Iranian god of light, had long celebrated December 25 as Mithra's birthday. December 21, being the winter solace, marked the beginning of days with increasing light, hence December 25 celebrated Mithra's triumph over darkness. Because the pagan festival that celebrated Mithra's birthday was so popular, the Roman Catholic church adopted the day, but changed the meaning from the birthday of Mithra, the god of light, to Christ's birthday!!! Nowhere in the Bible did the apostles or the early church celebrate the birthday of Jesus.

(3)
FALSE RELIGIONS ARE AN ABOMINATION TO GOD THE ROMAN CATHOLIC CHURCH - ON SAINTHOOD & MARY!!!

(Mark 7:6-9) Well hath Esaias prophesied of you hypocrites, as it is written, This people honors me with their lips, but their heart is far from me. In vain do they worship me, teaching the doctrines and commandments of men. Laying aside the commandment of God, ye hold the tradition of men, and many other such like things ye do. Full well ye reject the commandment of God, that ye may keep your own tradition.

There is much deception in these END TIMES, BEWARE! Concluding my study on Catholicism, please consider some more **NON-BIBLICAL** things they teach!

1) MORE ON THE VIRGIN MARY: Roman Catholics are taught that Mary is remained a virgin and never had sex after Jesus was born, denying that Jesus had brothers and sisters. **(See Matthew 1:24-25 & 13:55-56)**

2) MARY IS THE MEDIATOR BETWEEN GOD AND MAN: The Pope teaches that Mary is the mediator between God and man, not Christ! **(See 1 Timothy 2:5)** Catholics pray to Mary instead of God.to have their prayers answered. **(See Luke 11:27-28)**

(1Timothy 2:5) For there is one God, and one mediator between God and men, the man Christ Jesus.

3) ONLY SPECIAL DEAD CATHOLICS ARE DESIGNATED AS SAINTS: The Pope says only very special dead Catholic people qualify to be called saints.   For example, Pope John Paul II could not make Mother Teresa a saint (official canonization) until after she was dead. **(See 1 Corinthians 1:2; Ephesians 1:1; Romans 1:7)**

4) THE POPE CAN CHANGE THE BIBLE: In Catholicism, they teach and believe that the Pope can change what is in the Bible if he wants. Did Jesus say it was OK for man to change what the Word of God teaches for man-made Catholic doctrine? **(See Mark 7:7-9)**

PAGAN WORSHIP IS AN ABOMINATION TO GOD
(C)   MAYBE YOU WERE INVOLVED IN PAGAN RELIGIONS AND THEIR ABOMINATIONS

I am attempting in the following listing to list some of the primary false teachings and religions that are prevalent in these End Times! There are many others, I am sure, but the following are some of the major ones that have deceived and mislead multitudes! Please feel free to investigate the background of them! My purpose of listing them is to help you identify any practices or activities which could have caused you to stumble! If you are or have been involved in any of these listed, it could be a reason the Lord Jesus Christ left you behind when The Rapture took place!

African tribal worship; ancestor worship; Agnostic; Apostolic (be careful with their teachings can be misleading by emphasizing the teachings of Paul (or apostles doctrine, as superior to the (4) Gospels, the Revelation and the OT); – **(See Matt.4:4);**

Armstrong's (Worldwide Church of God; Astral Projection; Astrology; Atheism; Bahaism; Black Magic; Buddhism; Catholicism (See separate info); Christian Science; Clairvoyance; Crossroads Movement; Crystal Balls; Cursing Others; Deja-Vu; Demon worship; Divination; Divine Light Mission; Drug Trips; Dungeons and Dragons Game; Eastern Mysticism; Eastern Star; Enchantments or Fortune-telling; Evolution; ESP; Familiar Spirits; Fetishes; Fortune-telling; Masons, Freemasonry; Halloween, Hare Krishna; Hexing; Hinduism; Horoscopes; Humanism; Humanistic Philosophy; Hypnotism; I AM Movement; Idols -Ankh; Idols – Zodiac Signs; Idols – Italian Horn; Incantation; Indian ceremonies; Inner Peace Movement; Islam; Jehovah Witness; Job's Daughters; Kabbala; Knights of Columbus; KKK; Krishna Consciousness; Levitation; Magic; Charms, Casting Spells; Manipulation; Martial Arts; Mediums; Metaphysics; Mind Control; Mormonism (The Latter Day Saints); Moslems (same as Islam); New Age Thinking; New Age Doctrines; Numerology; Occultism; Ouija Boards; Palm Reading; Psychics, Satan Worship; Seances; Secret Societies; Secret Brotherhoods and Sisterhoods; Sorcery; and Witchcraft!

(D) MAYBE YOU WERE LEFT BEHIND BECAUSE YOUR FACINATION WITH DENOMINATIONAL AFFILIATION

(Romans 12:5) So we, being many, are one body in Christ, and everyone members one of another. (See 1Corinthians 12:13; Galatians 3:28; Ephesians 4:4-5; 5:27)

(1)
FALSE DOCTRINE IS A DECEPTION OF THE ENEMY
DENOMINATIONS ARE MAN-MADE ORGANIZATIONS

(Romans 12:5) says: So we, being many, are one body in Christ, and every one members one of another. (Read 1 Corinthians 12:12-14;18-20; 25) (Ephesians 4:4-6) There is one body, and one Spirit, even as you also were called in one hope of your calling; One Lord, one faith, one baptism, one God and Father of all, who is over all, and through all, and in us all.!

Religious sects are man-made groups/factions of DIVISION that view themselves as exalted ones, holding keys of understanding, standing separate and divided from the norm! Modern-day denominations are religious sects, like the ones Jesus encountered such as the Scribes, Pharisees and Sadducees!   Just as those sects were, today's denominations have opposing views of God and are divided in their beliefs and interpretation of God's Word.   Denominational affiliation did not enable you to be **Raptured** by Christ because it was irrelevant to Him!   Spiritually there was **ONLY ONE CHRISTIAN CHURCH**, not many! The Church was not an organization but a spiritual organism, it was the **MYSTICAL BODY OF CHRIST!**   Those that were Raptured WERE NOT COGIC, or BAPTIST, or DIVIDED, but CHRISTIANS, spiritually united with ALL CHRISTIANS who had been positioned/placed in the mystical BODY OF CHRIST by the Holy Spirit of God!   To become a part of the **BODY OF CHRIST** they made a spiritual transaction, which one makes with God by faith; all those taken had to make that transaction with God! One must repent of sin and accept Christ as Savior, and then the Holy Spirit spiritually places that individual into the **BODY OF CHRIST!**   There are approximately 41,000 Christian denominations, defined as religious groupings within a faith that have their own systems of organization based on division! Denominations are man-made organizations formed to attain power, wealth, control, position, and authority! But Jesus is **THE HEAD of HIS BODY, THE ONE CHRISTIAN CHURCH,** being His mystical body on earth, and **HE IS NOT DIVIDED** into separate and numerous denominations! In **the Rapture** that has taken place, Christ appeared in the air and retrieved **HIS BODY** or as the scripture says: **ALL THOSE WHO WERE IN HIM!**   Satan prompted the formation of denominations for the purpose of **weakening the Body of Christ,** instigating mental and spiritual opposition of each other! This activity was an attempt to reduce the Christian community into a **weakened state,** deactivating its ability to successfully engage in spiritual warfare against the forces of evil! I pull down this spiritual stronghold of division built in the minds of those who have been left behind who wish to be saved during this Great Tribulation period! My prayer today is for you to realize that all the true Christians taken in **The Rapture,** were those who made up the **ONE BODY IN CHRIST JESUS!**

MAYBE YOU WERE LEFT BEHIND BECAUSE

(E) <u>YOU LOVED THE WORLD MORE THAN YOU LOVE GOD</u>

<u>(1)</u>
<u>BEING WORLDLY IS UNACCEPTABLE TO GOD</u>
<u>WORLDLINESS AND IMMORALITY!</u>

(<u>1John 2:15</u>) Love not the world, neither the things that are in the world. If any man loves the world, the love of the Father is not in him.

Biblically, the world is the Satanic system along with its sinful activities which are aligned to rebel against the Will and Word of God! Having a love for the world and the things of the world separates us from the Love of God! We are living in a time when many professing Christianity are **WORLDLY** causing many of them to be left behind! The Bible says, **LOVE NOT THE WORLD, NEITHER THE THINGS IN THE WORLD**; to love the world, to put your trust in it, instead of in God, is damaging! **(See Matthew 6:19-24) ONE CANNOT LIVE IN WORLDLY LUST AND BE ACCEPTED BY GOD** for the love of the world and of God does not mix!!! By **THE WORLD** I mean aligning yourself with the ways, passions, pleasures and pursuits of the world! **(James 4:4)** illustrates that friendship with the world is friendship with the Prince of this World, Satan, who opposes Christ!!! Thus, one cannot love both God and **THE WORLD (See Matthew 6:24; 1John 2:16).** So, to love the world means the love of the Father is not in you! To those of you who fell prey to the **prosperity messages** which directed you to covet after worldly things, **SUCH IS OF THE SATANIC SYSTEM, NOT OF GOD! FOR YOUR TREASURE WAS SUPPOSE TO BE IN HEAVEN!!!**

> *(<u>1John 5:19</u>) And we know that we are of God, and the whole world lieth in wickedness.*
> *(<u>John 17:16</u>) They are not of the world, even as I am not of the world.*
> *(<u>Revelation 18:4</u>) And I heard another voice from heaven, saying, Come out of her, my people, that ye be not partakers of her sins, and that ye receive not of her plagues.*
> *(<u>James 4:4</u>) Ye adulterers and adulteresses, know ye not that the friendship of the world is enmity with God? Whosoever therefore will be a friend of the world is the enemy of God.*

Because the whole world lies in WICKEDNESS, it is hard to be

Righteous without sacrificing yourself to live for God!   The mindset of **THE WORLD** had even infiltrated into THE CHURCH!!! In these End Days, many in THE CHURCH were acting like those in **THE WORLD** AND NOT LIKE GOD!!! Minds are blurred regarding RIGHT and WRONG! Since the whole world lies in wickedness, and immorality the question you must ask is: are you on the right pathway? Ask yourself: ARE YOUR BELIEFS & ACTIVITIES IN ALIGNMENT WITH OR CONTRARY TO **THE WORLD**?

In **(John 17:16)** is a scripture out of the famous prayer that Jesus prayed for His Church!   Notice Christ did not pray that we might be rich and be great in this evil world, but that we might be kept from sin, strengthened, empowered, united, and brought safe to Heaven! **THE PROSPERITY OF THE SOUL IS THE BEST PROSPERITY**! Though in **THE WORLD,** you are not to be of, **THE WORLD!** Jesus prayed for the Father to keep His people from evil, from the corruption of **THE WORLD** and from the power of Satan!   You are not left here to pursue the same objects as those in **THE WORLD,** but to glorify God! The **Spirit of God** in **TRUE CHRISTIANS** is opposed to the **spirit of THE WORLD!** Now, if you have not aligned yourself with the mindset and will of God for your life and have been consumed with worldly lust; it could be a strong reason you have been left behind in **The Rapture!**

<u>WARNING: WORLD MIXING IS UNACCEPTABLE</u>! By the Spirit of God, I must tell you, IT IS NOT OKAY TO MIX WITH **THE WORLD,** NOT EVEN NOW IN THE GREAT TRIBULATION! Many who thought they were in the church were deceived, thinking it is okay to mix with sinners in their sinful activities and sinful lifestyles, well, it was and is not okay! Children of God were called be a light to **THE WORLD** and if you are of God, you are called to separate yourself from **THE WORLD** system of sin! Can't you hear Jesus say, **COME OUT OF HER MY PEOPLE AND BE NOT PARTAKERS OF HER SINS! (Revelation 18:4)**

<u>WARNING: RUN FROM THE WORLD</u>!   In these End Times many were running from the **TRUTH** of the Word of God, when they should have been running from **THE WORLD**

(The Satanic System)!   Instead of embracing worldly pleasures, behavior and activities you should been embracing **Godliness and Righteousness!** You see, **THE WORLD** hates the things OF GOD and **THE WORLD** will hate you if you are OF GOD! Here's a way to gauge your activities: IF **THE WORLD** LOVES IT, ACCEPTS IT, OR IS PARTICIPATING IN IT, IT IS NOT GOD! You cannot be a friend of **THE WORLD** and a friend of GOD!!!!

MAYBE YOU WERE LEFT BEHIND BECAUSE
(F)   <u>YOU WERE INVOLVED IN DEMONIC RITUALS</u>

(1)
<u>DEMON WORSHIP IS UNACCEPTABLE TO GOD</u>
<u>WARNNING! HALLOWEEN IS A PAGAN HOLIDAY!</u>

*(**Revelation 18:4**) I heard a voice from heaven, saying, Come out of her, my people, be not partakers of her sins, that ye receive not of her plagues.*

There are a couple of Demonic Rituals that are an **ABOMINATION TO OUR GOD**, that were prevalent in these End Days which I am being lead to illustrate! I have already discussed pagan holidays in section 5 of this chapter 10, but I wish to specifically deal further with **Halloween!** The reason being isthat it is widely accepted by the End Times world and is directly demonic in nature!   **Halloween** is the revival of an ancient satanic ritual that is tied to **THE WORSHIP OF DEMON ENTITIES OR THE WORSHIP OF DEVILS (See Rev. 9:20)**! **Halloween** originated in Ireland, annually observed on October 31, and is tied to pagan roots and dedicated to remembering **THE DEAD**! **Halloween** activities include **TRICK-OR-TREATING**: a form of ancient souling, where children and the poor sing and say prayers for the dead in return for treats!   **Halloween** COSTUMES are traditionally taken from frightening supernatural (demonic) or folkloric beings; representing that the souls of the dead have come into our world! The use of **PUMPKINS** for **Halloween** originated from an Irish myth about a man name Stingy Jack who supposedly used a cross to trap the Devil. **APPLE BOBBING** is tied to a Celtic pagan observance honoring the goddess of fruit trees, Pomona, a fertility goddess! You all know the other satanic symbols associated with **Halloween** which include **jack-o'-lanterns, bonfires, haunted attractions, pranks, and horror films! MY PRAYER IS THAT YOU COME OUT OF HER (THE WORLD'S SINS) AND COME TO THE WORD OF GOD – THAT YOU MAY BE SAVED FROM THE WRATH TO SOON COME!**

(2)
DEMON WORSHIP IS UNACCEPTABLE TO GOD
ABORTION – THE SACRIFICE OF THE UNBORN!

(<u>Leviticus 18:21</u>) And thou shalt not let any of thy seed pass through the fire to MOLECH, neither shalt thou profane the name of thy God: I am the LORD.

The other Demonic Ritual that is an **ABOMINATION TO OUR GOD and widely prominent during the end times,** is **ABORTIONS** tied to the **PRO-CHOICE MOVEMENT!** This act is spiritually **THE SACRIFICE OF THE INNOCENT TO AN EVIL SPIRIT** worshipping the ancient god **MOLECH,** an ancient Ammonite god **(a Fallen Angel)! MOLECH** -worship was practiced by the Canaanites and Phoenicians which caused God to send Israel into captivity **(See Amos 5:25-27).** The worship of **MOLECH** was associated with **child sacrifice** in which parents sacrificed or (killed) their children by causing them to **PASS THROUGH FIRE (See 2 Chronicles 28:3, 33:6; Jeremiah 7:31, 19:2–6)!** Today, children are sacrificed to **MOLECH** by **KILLING THEM IN THE WOMB!** Satan has revived ancient demon worship in many forms today, **BEWARE!** God brings forgiveness from past sin but, as you come into spiritual knowledge & understanding, turn from the practices of this evil world! If you were involved in such activity or have in the past, aborted a child, now that you have found out the truth, ask God to forgive you for such an act. If you ask God, He will forgive and cleanse you and this will open you up for God's Spirit to minister to your soul, allowing you acceptance for redemption!

CHAPTER 14
MAYBE YOU WERE LEFT BEHIND
BECAUSE YOU STRAYED FROM THE TRUTH!

WHAT THIS CHAPTER IS ABOUT
NOW THAT WE HAVE EXAMINED THINGS THAT DOESN'T MAKE YOU A
CHRISTIAN, I WISH TO BE MORE STRAIGHTFORWARD IN SOME OF THE PRIMARY
REASONS THAT YOU HAVE BEEN LEFT BEHIND! LET'S LOOK INTENSELY AT
THINGS THAT WASN'T BASED ON A LACK OF KNOWLEDGE BUT ON DECISIONS
MADE OR LACK THEREOF ON YOU PART!   IT IS UP TO THE INDIVIDUAL,
WHETHER THEY BE A SAINT OR SINNER, TO SEEK TRUTH AND TO ENSURE TO
KNOW THE TRUTH OF THE WORD FOR THEMSELVES. IN OTHER WORDS, IT WAS
UP TO YOU TO FOLLOW CHRIST AND NOT MEN! GOD GIVES US ALL FREE WILL
TO DECIDE WHOM WE WILL SERVE! LET'S LOOK AT SOME OF THESE THINGS!

(A)   MAYBE YOU STRAYED FROM THE TRUTH
AND WOULD NOT ENDURE SOUND DOCTRINE

*(2 Timothy 4:3-4) For the time will come when they will not ENDURE
SOUND DOCTRINE; but after THEIR OWN LUST shall they heap to
themselves teachers, having itching ears; They SHALL TURN AWAY
THEIR EARS FROM THE TRUTH, and shall be turned unto fables
(LIES).*
*(2Thessalonians 2:10-11) And with all deceivableness of
unrighteousness in them that perish; because they received not THE
LOVE OF THE TRUTH that they might be saved! And for this cause
God shall send them strong delusion, that they should believe a lie:*

THE BIBLE SAYS THE TIME WILL COME in the End of
Time, **WHEN PEOPLE WOULD NOT BE ABLE TO
ENDURE SOUND DOCTRINE** (True Gospel Teaching, the
doctrine which imparts Godliness)! The word **endure** biblically
means that there will be people who would not be able to tolerate,
to bear, or accept **SOUND DOCTRINE OR THE TRUTH** as
revealed in the Word of God!   Yes, we are in the End of Time and
there were numerous professing Christians who could not endure
(tolerate, stomach, or bear) Sound Doctrine!   These people heap
upon themselves (lust after), leaders/teachers who are acceptable
to worldliness, preach a **non-convicting gospel** and **who do not**
condemn their sins! The Bible continues to say they will have
'itching ears,' meaning they will shun **THE TRUE LEADERS
OF CHRIST** and they seek out new defined moralities and

churches that will sensationalize, amuse and flatter them!   These individuals **RUN TO FALSE TEACHERS** who **WILL NOT CONDEMN THEIR SINS** and they will **run from** - **THE TRUE TEACHERS OF CHRIST that CONDEMN SIN!** The Bible says because they have **'itching ears,'** they have desire for new doctrines, being in an atmosphere that is pleasing and entertaining to their flesh and that doesn't make demands such as true righteousness and submission to God's Word!   They love to hear fables or stories, myths, even lies, things that will humor them, not any word that offends them! When the truth of God's Word is given, they are agitated and disturbed and turn away their ears from the truth!   Could it be that they think they could hear it and receive it and possibly must submit to it?   These people hate the demands of The Word of God because it condemns their lifestyles! They are opened to accept **LIES**, and thus allow themselves to be captured to disregard the **Will of God** for **true redemption!** Before **the Rapture** took place, there were many individuals that fit this exact description, which is why many of them, if not all of them, were **LEFT FBEHIND!**

(B) MAYBE YOU STRAYED FROM THE TRUTH AND DID NOT WANT TO SUBMIT TO THE WORD OF GOD

(2Timothy 4:4) And they shall turn away their ears from the truth and shall be turned unto fables.

In these **END DAYS** there were many who professed Christianity but refused to accept **THE TRUTH OF GOD'S WORD**! Many inside church assemblies closed their ears and their minds, redirected their eyesight, sought to avoid reading and studying the Word of God, became agitated, would argue with you on your interpretation, and in all actuality, ran from the truths of it! Many did not want to know what God was really saying and had a short attention span when God's name or word was discussed! Just before The Rapture, a Pastor could not speak regarding sinful conduct, could not rebuke anyone regarding sinful behavior, could not chastise, correct, give counsel on righteousness, reprimand, or overly mention Jesus!   Satan had established a mindset in many End Time churchgoers that what God says isn't applicable (relevant, appropriate, or valid) to them and the times they live in! They said God was doing a 'new thing' and they wished to do what they wanted, regardless of what the Word of God says!   But the Bible says in these last days people will be **TURNING FROM THE TRUTH,** because they will want to profess Christianity, but still live lifestyles which are against the directives God makes through His Word!   The preference in these End Times seems to be that any communication in the end time churches was acceptable except the communication of truth!   God-imparted truth seemed to cause a turning away of the eyes and ears of those who did not, in their heart, wish to truly serve Him!   **ALL OF THESE WERE LEFT BEHIND!**

(C)   MAYBE YOU STRAYED FROM THE TRUTH AND HAD YOUR OWN DEFINITION OF WHAT A CHRISTIAN WAS

We are living in the End of Time and The Rapture has occurred!   But we are also living in a time when many have been deceived by that which is false! There is confusion as to what True Christianity is!   Satan, through the false prophets (false preachers & teachers) has mixed the world with the church and many professing Christians are drinking the lies in the mix! In many church assemblies, all restrictions were lifted and it was hard to tell if you are in a Church Service or The Club!   Many professing Christians in these ends of days can't stand any hardship or lack, have bought into the prosperity false ministries, live in lust and gratification of their flesh, and have conformed their dress & activities to reflect the world instead of God!

> Jesus said in *(Revelation 3:18): I counsel thee to buy of me gold tried in the fire, that thou mayest be rich; and white raiment, that thou mayest be clothed, and that the shame of thy nakedness do not appear; and anoint thine eyes with eye-salve, that thou mayest see.(KJV)*

So, why are many being deceived? BECAUSE THEY LOVE NOT THE TRUTH BUT WOULD RATHER BELIEVE A LIE (untruths)! My Brothers and Sisters, in order to attain the Kingdom of God, you must love truth, because IT IS TRUTH THAT WILL MAKE YOU FREE AND LEAD YOU HOME! BE WARNED, BE CAREFUL, BE WATCHFUL, BE CAUTIOUS, -- THE WAR IS STILL BEING FOUGHT FOR YOUR SOUL!!!!!!

(D)   MAYBE YOU STRAYED FROM THE TRUTH

<u>AND WERE MISLEAD UNDER FALSE LEADERSHIP</u>

(<u>Colossians 2:8</u>) Beware lest any man spoil you through philosophy and vain deceit, after the tradition of men, after the rudiments of the world, and not after Christ.

The Bible warns that in **The Last Days** there would be an enormous increase of that which is FALSE, FALSE PREACHERS & TEACHERS who are compromising and are progressing **FALSE DOCTRINES!** I warned the people of God to take to heart **(Colossians 2:8)** and **BEWARE!!!** Lest any man spoil you or (pamper) you; through man-made doctrines, making plunder of you; robbing you of spiritual blessings by leading you to depend on something besides Christ for your stability and your salvation! False leadership will be based on **The Rudiments of the World**, mixing the message of Christ with worldly things such as materialism, wealth, and prosperity; mixing it with the Mosaic ceremonies (the OT Law of works), in comparison and in correlation with the Gospel of Christ (NT Doctrine of Faith through Grace)! Jesus Christ did give His life for all who will accept salvation, but once accepted, we are called to a higher standard, a separation from the world, to walk in obedience to His Word and His will! We are not to continue in the old sinful lifestyle of the past of which the false leaders deceitfully promote! Christians are to be new creatures in Christ, old things have passed away and all things have become new! Many have been left behind because they have been blind followers of leaders who are not worthy to be Ministers of Christ! The Apostle Paul not only preached the Gospel of Jesus Christ but lived a life of not compromising the Word of God! Any leader that does not stand on the Word of God is not worthy to be a Minister of Christ and should not be followed! Your leader should be a perfect example of strict obedience to God's Word, as related in the Scriptures! Our worship is to God, who is unseen, not to man who is seen! Every Church leader should say as the Apostle Paul said, follow me as I follow Christ!

(E) MAYBE YOU STRAYED FROM THE TRUTH <u>AND THOUGHT GOD WAS DOING A NEW THING</u>

(<u>Isaiah 46:10</u>) Declaring the end from the beginning, and from ancient times the things that are not yet done, saying, My counsel shall stand, and I will do all my pleasure:

The false leaders preach the lie that God is doing something new and changes with the times! But remember, just before Jesus died on the cross He said, **IT IS FINISHED!** What is or can be new to God that will require Him to have to modify His declared Word or methods? WHAT GOD HAS SAID AND HAS SPOKEN WILL STAND FOREVER, HE DOESN'T HAVE TO CHANGE IT! God is not doing a NEW THING, accommodating sinful men and women and adapting His Plan to appease them and their fleshly appetites! The Plan of God was forged from the foundation of the world and He knew THE END in THE BEGINNING, therefore no revisions, corrections or modifications are required! The Word of God is everlasting to everlasting, Heaven and Earth shall pass away but the Word of God shall never pass away!

(F)   MAYBE YOU STRAYED FROM THE TRUTH AND BELIEVED THE CHURCH WAS A MONEY GENERATING ENTERPRISE

> *(John 2:14-16) He made a scourge of small cords, drove them all out of the temple, & the sheep, & the oxen; & poured out the changers' money, & overthrew the tables*
> *(Matthew 10:8) Heal the sick, cleanse the lepers, raise the dead, cast out devils: FREELY YE HAVE RECEIVED, FREELY GIVE!*
> *(Matthew 21:12-13) And said unto them, It is written, My house shall be called the house of prayer; but ye have made it a den of thieves.*

In this, the End of the Age false Christian Churches has become a **DEN OF THIEVES! At the End of the Ages** we have seen the Commercialization of the Church! Please let me stress to you that the source of the **SPIRITUAL WORK OF GOD --- IS GOD!** The things of God are spiritual in nature and **NOT OF THIS WORLD**, therefore spiritual knowledge & abilities are given by God to those who are called by Him to perform **HIS WORK!** To take the things of God and commercialize them and see them for personal gain is an abomination! God says in the above scripture to not attach a price to His work! But today, to the contrary, many individuals in the end of the Age would not render ministry work unless paid! Preachers would not preach, musicians would not play, teachers would not teach, janitors would not even clean the sanctuaries with being paid!

Let us notice that Jesus in the **BEGINNING & END OF HIS MINISTRY** drove the **MERCHANDISERS** out of the temple and overthrew their tables. The primary emphasis in the church today is MONEY rather than GOD! In the above scripture ***JESUS PERFORMED A CLEANSING OF THE TEMPLE***!!! Jesus drove the **MERCHANDISERS** out of the temple and overthrew their tables!!! He recognized them as using the temple for worldly gain, the desecration and defilement of the House of Prayer! Jesus went into the temple at the start and finish of His ministry for the purpose of cleansing the temple!!!   He did this by driving them all out and overturning their money tables!   The **ENDTIME** Traffickers of today are persistent in their lust for money, from selling the Word of God to preaching Old Testament tithes to the New Testament Church; they are merchandising the people!!! Yes, preachers in the end days are saying that your money is the seed that you plant to give you right standing with God!   But the real fact is it brings in the money for their salaries!   That message of worldly and carnal prosperity (carnal blessings) has caused many to lose their way and be **LEFT BEHIND!**

> ***(Matthew 6:19-20) Lay not up for yourselves treasures upon earth, where moth and rust doth corrupt, and where thieves break through and steal: But lay up for yourselves treasures in Heaven, where neither moth nor rust doth corrupt, and where thieves do not break through nor steal:***

The exchange of money, the selling, and commercializing in the Houses of Prayer are an abomination in the eyesight of God! The CHURCH is supposed to be a place of sacred worship but instead it has become a den of thieves or a cave or den of robbers! The language indicates that it creates corrupt and fraudulent traffic, which corrupt and fraudulent leadership has permitted to encroach on the worship of God.   For Jesus to drive them out of the temple at the BEGINNING and END of His ministry is significant and reveals the disdain God has for merchandising in His temple!   The voice of the Master has been ignored in these Last Days because MONEY is the focus in the End Time Church!!! Did not Jesus say,

Make not My Father's House a House of Merchandise??? DID HE NOT SAY, YOU, (The False Prophets), HAVE MADE IT A DEN OF THIEVES!!!!

(G)   MAYBE YOU STRAYED FROM THE TRUTH BECAUSE YOU WERE INSINCERE, SELFISH, AND FULL OF HATRED

Now you should evaluate if you are a selfish and hateful person or are you a person that is full of love and harmony with mankind? In order to be able to receive the Spirit of God, and in order to receive Christ, you must be of a pure heart, loving and kind and submissive to God for the life of the Lord Jesus Christ to dwell in you! When I say having a pure heart, I mean you must be real and not fake or false, not have an insincere reason for wanting Christ in your life! The reason is this: God knows your heart, intents, motives and nothing can be hidden from Him! If you truly desire Christ in your life and sincerely desire Him as Savior, God knows it! So, your heart must be pure to open your spirit up to receive the Spirit of Christ!

(__Matthew 5:8__) Blessed are the pure in heart: for they shall see God.

__Blessed are__ **the pure in heart**. Pure in heart; is a heart wants to be free from the dominion and pollution of sin.
They shall see God; Shall be opened to have right views of Him and enjoy His presence here and hereafter.
Let me repeat the fact that you cannot have corrupt motives in desiring the in-dwelling of Christ! Those who are false, care little for the state of the heart, keeping an outward form of goodness are unacceptable to God! Jesus, however, demands that the heart, the affections, the mind, be sincere; they are the fountain from whence flows the moral and true foundation for the Christian life. A pure heart begets a pure life, an impure heart, a corrupt life. Only the

pure in heart shall see God, shall be open to see the reality of the Kingdom of Heaven!   The Kingdom of Heaven cannot be seen with the natural eye, but only with spiritual vision, by faith.   In the pure heart the Lord will dwell, and His presence will be recognized.

> *(<u>John 14:23</u>) Jesus answered and said unto him, If a man love me, he will keep my words: and my Father will love him, and we will come unto him, and make our abode with him.*

Love of Jesus Christ will lead you to obey His commands, and will secure to you the illuminating, purifying, and blissful presence of both the Father and the Son.   You shall dwell with Him and He with you, and your habitual communion can be truly with the Father and His Son Jesus Christ. **(1John 1:3).**

> *(<u>Revelation 3:17</u>) You say, I am rich, increased with goods, & have need of nothing; YOU KNOW NOT that you are wretched, miserable, poor, blind, & naked!*

In **The Release of Spiritual Knowledge,** let's examine the spiritual aspect of scripture! **Selfishness** defined is self-interest, greed, and egotism! But the true definition of **Selfishness** is **SPIRITUAL IGNORANCE!**   **Selfishness** is being oblivious to one's true condition **(cannot see yourself)!** There are numerous reasons for professing Christians to be selfish, but the primary reason is refusal to seek the truth of God's Word!   Many today are led by denominational doctrines, doctrines of men, & doctrines of devils; absolutely refusing to study the Word of God for themselves!   The self-life is lived to please one's self rather than God!   The pleasing of self **DENIES THE SACRIFICE REQUIRED** for true dedication to God!   Self-limits the extent of commitment TO GOD but demands full commitment FROM GOD!   **PLEASING SELF RATHER THAN GOD MEANS ONE IS MISDIRECTED AND DOESN'T KNOW IT!**

<u>If you hate others because of their race, or if you are a</u>

<u>**bigot, or if you practice discrimination against others you are
working with Satan – and you are employing A DEMONIC
SPIRIT OF OPPRESSION!**</u>

*(1 John 2:9) He that says he is in the light, & hates his brother, is in
darkness!*

**THIS MESSAGE IS DIRECTLY TO THOSE WHO
PROFESS TO BE A CHRISTIAN AND ARE INWARDLY
RACE HATERS!** This is not a feeling that comes from God,
but this disposition comes from Satan in the form of **a demon
spirit of oppression!** Would you like to be oppressed in the
manner you are oppressing others? When I say racist or racism I
am also talking about a mindset and activities affiliated with bigotry
and discrimination! No person practicing racism and
discrimination will enter the Kingdom of Heaven, you are doomed
to the Lake of Fire if you do not ask God to forgive you and
cleanse you! Repent while you have time! Examine yourself if you
still want a chance to be saved in this **TRIBULATION
PERIOD,** for God will not accept you if you hold these feelings in
your heart! Many racists are deceitful, known to lie and not admit
that they feel this way about other races, but God knows your
heart! Racism is based on hatred. Hatred is tied to **THE WORLD**
which is tied to **THE SATANIC SYSTEM.** Racism is an activity
of Satan for he is the Father of Hatred, he hates God! Children of
God should not exercise any type of race hatred! The Bible clearly
asserts that all humankind, whether Black, White, Hispanic, Asian,
mixed-race or any other race -- is the work of God, the Creator's
hands. In the Bible, God doesn't make distinctions based on
physical or social attributes. God does not look at the outward
appearance, but the Lord looks at the heart. **(See 1 Samuel 16:7)**
The Bible tells us to consider others before ourselves! God
encourages people to treat others with respect and dignity. In the
Apostle Paul's letter to the church at Philippi, he tells the new
believers, in humility, value others above yourselves, not looking to
your own interests but each of you to the interests of the others.
**(See Philippians 2:3-4) ONE CANNOT BE A CHRISTIAN
AND BE RACIST!!!**

(H)   MAYBE YOU STRAYED FROM THE TRUTH AND FELL AWAY FROM THE FAITH

(2Thessalonians 2:3) Let no man deceive you by any means: for that day shall not come, except there comes a falling away first, and that man of sin be revealed, the son of perdition;

What we see today is that many professing Christianity were left behind when Jesus came and Raptured His Church and many of them did not realize that they had become opposed to Biblical Truth and the Doctrine of Christ! In these End Times there was a great **falling away**: a great apostasy, there is a refusal to accept Christian beliefs as taught by the Word of God, a transition from the faith and practice of the Gospel! To make it more plain to you, the false teachers were teaching doctrines that were not true,. They taught that you could connect with God by what you do and not by **WHAT CHRIST HAD DONE FOR YOU!**   The simple truth is your belief in God had to be by faith and all through Christ Jesus!   Not of works lest any man should boast, it is a gift of God! Faith working with Grace is what Christianity is all about!   Grace (meaning your salvation) and all things received from God is a gift of God!   The Apostle Paul stated that just before the Son of Perdition (The Anti-Christ) is revealed, there shall be a general falling away from the purity of the faith. There shall be a gradual declining, corruption, and departure from righteousness by those professing to be Children of God! Remember, faith without works are dead! **(Read James 2:18-26)**

(I)   MAYBE YOU STRAYED FROM THE TRUTH AND WERE DECEIVED ABOUT THE ORDER OF GOD FOR THE CHURCH

(1Timothy 3:2)   "A bishop then must be blameless, the husband of one wife, vigilant, sober, of good behavior, given to hospitality, apt to teach;"
(1Timothy 3:12) "Let the deacons be the husbands of one wife, ruling their children and their own houses well."
(1Timothy 2:12) "But I suffer not a woman to teach, nor to usurp authority over the man, but to be in silence."

In these End Times women in the Christian Church have been seduced by Satan to want to be like the man, or equal to a man!   That may be an okay way in 'the world' but in the Body of

Christ, there is an order ordained by God! Though Eve was taken out of the side of man, her being deceived by Satan caused her to come under the dominion of the man and God never reversed that order. In the above scriptures you see God indicates men as Bishops, Deacons, teachers, and all of Christ's disciples were men! When the Bible speaks of lineage, it never mentions women, all the major and minor prophets were men, as well as all the Kings of Israel. God says in the above scriptures for the church, 'the husband of one wife' not the wife of one husband. But women in these end days have diverted God's word to do the things they want to do in the Church, bringing the mindset of the world into the church and this could be the cause many are left behind!

So, why is God giving man the lead over women? Because of the following scriptures:

> **_(1Timothy 2:13)_ _"For Adam was first formed, then Eve."_**
> **_(1Timothy 2:14)_ _"And Adam was not deceived, but the woman being deceived was in the transgression."_**

Was in the transgression meaning the cause of the transgression for the fall of mankind! Some reasons drawn from the story of man and woman in Eden are given for these rules. It will be seen that Apostle Paul regards these events as shadowing forth spiritual lessons and directives. **Adam was first formed**. Man came in order before woman. Adam being formed first is an indication that he is the head of the woman, and that the office of teaching and governing belongs to him.

> **_(1Corinthians 11:8-9)_ _"For the man is not of the woman; but the woman of the man. Neither was the man created for the woman; but the woman for the man."_**

The apostle has reference to the public assemblies of believers. **(Compare 1Corinthians 14:34-35),** 'Let your women keep silence in the churches.' I do not care what women say, when it comes to the Christian Church and God's Word, they should be asking themselves: "Am I violating these scriptures?" "How is Christ going to take it if I am in violation with His Word?" You could be left behind!

CHAPTER 15
A STUDY ON THE FIRST RESURRECTION

WHAT THIS CHAPTER IS ABOUT

This is the pinnacle Chapter of the Book! Biblical teachings on The First Resurrections must be understood for you to understand the disappearance of a vast number of people from planet earth!   If you are familiar with the spiritual doctrine of Jesus Christ, you know that there are designated two (2) Resurrections, the First and the Second Resurrection!   THE FIRST RESURRECTION is what I wish to focus on in this chapter and is associated with gathering, by Christ, of the Righteous; in which Christ will gather every righteous soul from Adam to The Rapture of His Church!   I will briefly talk to the Second Resurrection but it will not be the focus of this chapter.

The purpose of **The First Resurrection** is to **gather all the righteous** and usher them into eternity to forever be with God!   In the **First Resurrection** the righteous dead as well as the righteous living are gathered by Christ and changed from mortal to immortal and then taken into the eternal Heavenly Realms of Glory!!! In this Chapter I will go into a Biblical Study of what **The First Resurrection** is and how it will play into your redemption is you follow the directives I give you from the Word of God regarding those who were Left Behind and not taken in The Rapture!

The Second Resurrection, which is not being covered in this book because my prayer is that it doesn't affect you, is the gathering of **the wicked** from Adam to the end of the Great Tribulation, in which God the Father will gather every wicked individual to stand before His Great White Throne for judgment and final sentence into the Lake of Fire!

> ***(John 5:29)   And shall come forth; they that have done good, unto the resurrection of life; and they that have done evil, unto the resurrection of damnation.***
> ***(John 5:28-29)   Marvel not at this: for the hour is coming, in the which all that are in the graves shall hear His voice,***
> ***And shall come forth; they that have done good, unto the***

resurrection of life; and they that have done evil, unto the resurrection of damnation.
(Revelation 20:6) Blessed and holy is he that hath part in The First Resurrection: on such the Second Death hath no power, but they shall be priests of God and of Christ, and shall reign with Him a thousand years.

THE RESURRECTION OF LIFE IS THE FIRST RESURRECTION OR THE RESURRECTION OF THE RIGHTEOUS!

THE RESURRECTION OF DAMNATION is **THE SECOND RESURRECTION** OR **THE RESURRECTION OF THE WICKED!**

It is relevant at this stage for me to revisit in your mind that there is an ancient spiritual war going on between God and Satan and that it has come to a climax in what you are now in: **THE GREAT TRIBULATION**! As forestated in earlier chapters, God's final plan is the elimination of all wickedness from His creations, thus cleansing and restoring His complete dominion! From the beginning, before the world was, God planned to bring the rebellion of evil to consummation and restore His creation back into harmony and peace!

Since it not my purpose in this book to address the events that will affect the wicked in **The Great Tribulation,** I reiterate my focus from the start was to give you understanding in what Christ shall accomplish in gathering His own, the righteous! Now let us take a detailed look at **The First Resurrection!**

THE FIRST RESURRECTION, OR THE RESURRECTION OF ALL THE RIGHTEOUS, IS BEING ACCOMPLISHED BY JESUS CHRIST IN THREE (3) PHASES!

ALL TAKEN IN THE FIRST RESURRECTION ARE BLESSED

__(Revelation 20:6)__ Blessed and holy is he that hath part in the first resurrection: on such the second death hath no power, but they shall be priests of God and of Christ, and shall reign with Him a thousand years.

Blessed and holy is he that hath part in The First Resurrection; this great moral and spiritual resurrection that brings in the Millennium Reign of Christ. On such, the second death (which is the final punishment of the wicked in The Lake of Fire) hath no power. The second death is the sad doom of eternal death. All the Saints that have been glorified will **Reign with Jesus for one thousand years and afterward, shall live in the realms of light with God for eternity**! Whether these thousand years are to be understood literally, or as a symbol of some mightier period, I am unable to determine, but I believe it as the Bible says 1000 years of Christ and the Saints ruling the planet! Here is an account of the reign of the saints, for the same space of time as Satan is bound. Those who have suffered with Christ, shall reign with Him in His spiritual and Heavenly Kingdom, in conformity to Him in His wisdom, righteousness, and holiness: this is called the First Resurrection, with which none but those who serve Christ, and suffer for Him, shall be favored. The happiness of these servants of God is declared. None can be blessed but those that are holy; and all that are holy shall be blessed. We know something of what the first death is, and it is very awful; but we know not what this Second Death is. It must be much more dreadful; it is the death of the soul, eternal separation from God. May you never know what it is: those who have been made partakers of a spiritual resurrection, are saved from the power of the Second Death. We stand in expectation of a thousand years that will follow the destruction of the Anti-Christ and, idolatrous, persecuting power; during which pure Christianity; in doctrine, worship, and holiness, will be made known over all the earth. By the all-powerful working of the Holy Spirit, fallen man will be created new; and faith and holiness will as certainly prevail, as unbelief and unholiness now do. We may easily perceive what a variety of dreadful pains, diseases, and other calamities would cease, if all men and women were true and consistent Christians. All the evils of public and private contests would be ended, and happiness of every kind largely increased. Every man and woman would try to lighten suffering, instead of adding to the sorrows. I pray for the promised glorious days, and I pray that you are strengthened in the Power of the Holy Spirit to choose Jesus in the coming dark and dreadful days ahead! Let's begin our study and look at the full scope of what The Lord, Jesus Christ is accomplishing in **THE 3 PHASES OF THE FIRST RESURRECTION!**

PHASE ONE (1) OF:
"THE FIRST RESURRECTION"
Termed The Gathering of The First Fruits: (Matthew 27:52-55)

(Matthew 27:52-53) And the graves were opened; and many bodies of the saints which slept arose, And came out of the graves after His resurrection, and went into the holy city, and appeared unto many.

After His resurrection from the dead, the scripture says many bodies of the saints which slept arose from the dead and went into the holy city and appeared to many as a witness that Jesus had risen and obtained the power over death! This scripture cannot be fully understood as to what transpired after they rose, but what I do know is they were a witness to the risen Christ! Now, before the resurrection of Jesus from the dead, it is a biblical fact that He went into the prison house of hell and set the captive free, this is found in:

(Psalms 24:7) Lift up your heads, O ye gates; and be ye lift up, ye everlasting doors; and the King of glory shall come in.

-------PHASE 1 OF THE FIRST RESURRECTION IS CALLED THE GATHERING OF 'THE FIRST FRUITS' or the beginning of the gathering of the righteous by The Lord Jesus Christ!   Let me start by telling you that all the events of the **Phase 1 of THE FIRST RESURRECTION** has already occurred, the gathering of the righteous souls from Adman to The Rapture! Now understand, before Jesus conquered death and hell the spirits of the righteous were housed in a paradise compartment of Hell and could not be set free until Jesus conquered and set them free by releasing them from Satan's confinement!   Yes, the righteous were confined in a paradise section of Hell because Satan, the god of this world, had the power of death and hell, and obtained the right to imprison all those that commit sin!   This means he has the power to hold the souls or spirits of men, women, even boys and girls who are passed the age of accountability, in the prison house of Hell because the wages of sin is death! The victory of our Lord Jesus Christ over death and hell was a victory for not only for Himself but also for the Old Testament Righteous and the New Testament Church, all who believe in Him!   Because God has shown Him the path of life, He would show it to them also that are united to Him by faith!

In this 1st Phase of **THE FIRST RESURRECTION** that I am conveying to you Jesus gathered or retrieved individual souls or spirits of those who are termed **THE FIRST FRUITS!** Jesus released the spirits of all those who died righteous from Adam up until the time of His resurrection and raised and released them all out of The Prison House of Hell, taking their spirits into an Heavenly Paradise, a place of rest and joy!   The scriptures tells us that Jesus, when His spirit entered Hell after His death on the cross, He preached to all of the spirits confined there, spirits of humans all the way back to Adam and Noah, because they had not heard of Christ or the Gospel, thus Jesus gave all humanity up to that point who were confined in Hell an opportunity to hear the Gospel and believe and be saved or release with Him when He rose! These are **THE FIRST FRUITS** gathered in Phase 1 of **THE FIRST RESURRECTION!**

Look carefully at the following scriptures:

> ***(1 Peter 3:18-20)** For Christ also suffered once for sins, the righteous for the unrighteous, to bring you to God. He was put to death in the body but made alive in the Spirit. [19]After being made alive, He went and made proclamation to the imprisoned spirits- [20]to those who were disobedient long ago when God waited patiently in the days of Noah while the ark was being built. In it only a few people, eight in all, were saved through water,*

> ***(1 Peter 4:4-6)** They are surprised that you do not join them in their reckless, wild living, and they heap abuse on you. [5]But they will have to give account to Him who is ready to judge the living and the dead. [6]For this is the reason the Gospel was preached even to those who are now dead, so that they might be judged according to human standards regarding the body but live according to God regarding the spirit.*

Though their bodies were still in the grave, Jesus took them to a Heavenly Paradise with Him when He rose from the dead, but their bodies would not be left there forever! For Christ appeared in the air, bringing with Him the spirits of **THE FIRST FRUITS, as He g**athered His Church in **Phase 2 of THE FIRST RESURRECTION**! And all who have died in Him shall retrieve their mortal bodies and be raised up incorruptible and glorious. For this corruptible must put on incorruption, and this mortal must put on immortality

> ***(1Corinthians 15:53).** For this corruptible must put on incorruption, and this mortal must put on immortality.*

In the coming millennial age, a more glorious order of society awaits the world than our darkened understandings are able to conceive of; and this will be but an earnest of the perfect redemption of Heaven, where God will in the fullest sense of the words swallow up death forever, and wipe away tears from off all faces. The kind reception of repentant sinners is often in the New

Testament likened to a feast. The guests invited are all people, Gentiles as well as Jews. There is that in the gospel which strengthens and makes glad the heart and is fit for those who are under convictions of sin, and mourning for it. There is a veil spread over all nations, for all sat in darkness. But this veil the Lord will destroy, by the light of His gospel shining in the world, and the power of His Spirit opening men's eyes to receive it. He will raise those to spiritual life who were long dead in trespasses and sins. Christ will Himself, in **THE FIRST RESURRECTION, triumph** over death. Grief shall be banished; there shall be perfect and endless joy. Those that mourn for sin shall be comforted. Those who suffer for Christ shall have consolations. But in the joys of Heaven, and not short of them, will fully be brought to pass this saying, God shall wipe away all tears **(Revelation 7:17; 21:4)!** Sometimes, in this world God takes away the reproach of His people from among men; however, it will be done fully at the Great Day when all the Righteous shall be brought home. **I encourage you, though you have been left behind, to patiently bear sorrow and shame now; both will be done away shortly, for God still wants to bring you to Himself, if you will obey His Word, you shall be brought into His glorious presence!**

PHASE TWO (2) OF:
"THE FIRST RESURRECTION"
Termed The Gathering of The Harvest: (1 Thessalonians 4:16-17)

***(1Thessalonians 4:16-17)** For the Lord Himself shall descend from heaven with a shout, with the voice of the archangel, and with the trump of God: and the dead in Christ shall rise first: Then we which are alive and remain shall be caught up together with them in the clouds, to meet the Lord in the air: and so shall we ever be with the Lord.*

PHASE 2 OF THE FIRST RESURRECTION IS CALLED THE HARVEST or Gathering by The Lord Jesus

Christ, aka, **THE RAPTURE** of the righteous who come from the seed of The Gospel of Christ!   Many in the Christian Church have disappeared and **<u>many professing Christianity have been left behind!</u>** To say it another way; true Christians have disappeared from the face of the earth, and the graves of all true Christians have been opened and their remains are gone! What the world has witnessed is **Phase 2 of** THE **FIRST RESURRECTION where the Lord Jesus Christ has appeared in the air and has Raptured His Church and sadly, you have been left behind! His Church is comprised of the Saints from after the Resurrection of Jesus 2000 years ago to the End Time Church!   This event happened in a moment, in a twinkling of an eye; it happened instantaneous, suddenly, without warning and the event is termed THE HARVEST or THE RAPTURE!**

<u>For the Lord Himself.</u> Jesus Christ Himself has come for His people, has come for the faithful, has come for those who are in His Body, His Church, those who have truly been born-again, both the living and those who have died in Him before His return! His descend from Heaven which will be in the air, or in the atmosphere above the earth, in the sky! He comes with a shout, with the voice of an archangel, the voice of command and the trump of God! The trumpet blast will sound as a signal and a summons! He will call forth His people, His sheep, saying:

(<u>Matthew 25:34</u>)   *Then shall the King say unto them on His right hand, Come, ye blessed of My Father, inherit the Kingdom prepared for you from the foundation of the world:*

For He had gone to prepare a place for us and now He has come so that where He is there we may be also!   The dead in Christ, (or the departed Saints), rose first. In that day, the first act was the gathering of the departed Saints; shoes bodies slept in-Christ; the next, the gathering of the living Saints!   I know you were not taken, but I want you to understand how the event happened!

> **_(1Corinthians 15:52-55)_ _In a moment, in the twinkling of an eye, at the last trump: for the trumpet shall sound, and the dead shall be raised incorruptible, and we shall be changed. For this corruptible must put on incorruption, and this mortal must put on immortality. So, when this corruptible shall have put on incorruption, and this mortal shall have put on immortality, then shall be brought to pass the saying that is written, Death is swallowed up in victory. O death, where is thy sting? O grave, where is thy victory?_**

Here it speaks at 'the last trump' which I feel is an indicator that this event would take place at the last trump or when we see the sign or the time of The Last Trump – President Donald Trump!   **The scripture goes on to say** for this corruptible body of flesh that all the Saints resided in while on planet earth was changed!   For this corruptible body gave place to an incorruptible body; the mortal frame to an immortal one. The righteous Saints put off one - mortality and put on the other - immortality. Then all the righteous of God were glorified; when the dead have been raised, and the living so changed as to fit them to live and reign with Christ in the Realms of Glory! The saying, was fulfilled that is written in.

> **_(Isaiah 25:8)_ _He will swallow up death in victory; and the Lord GOD will wipe away tears from off all faces; and the rebuke of His people shall He take away from off all the earth: for the LORD hath spoken it._**

The term **Rapture** is especially useful in discussing or disputing the exact timing or the scope of the event, particularly when asserting the pre-tribulation view that the rapture will occur before, not during, the Second Coming, with or without an extended Tribulation period.   There are differing views among Christians regarding the timing of Christ's return, such as whether it will occur in one event or two, and the meaning of the aerial gathering described in **(1 Thessalonians 4)**.   Many Christians do not subscribe to rapture-oriented theological views, though the term rapture is derived from the text of the Latin Vulgate of **(1**

Thessalonians 4:17), we will be caught up! I believed **THE RAPTURE** took place during the time that President Donald Trump was in office!   Since I am gone in the Rapture, only you can determine if I was right or not! This book is being written actually for two (2) purposes: one (1) to help prepare Christians to meet the Lord if the Rapture hasn't already occurred and two (2) to identify the processes one must take to still be saved if you have been left behind and find yourself in "The Great Tribulation!" So, if Phase Two (2), The Rapture, has taken place, know that there is only Phase Three (3) of the First Resurrection left!   Let us examine it with extreme seriousness, for it is the last gathering of the righteous by the Lord, Jesus Christ!

PHASE THREE (3) OF:
"THE FIRST RESURRECTION"
Termed The Gathering of The Gleanings: (Revelation 7:14; 20:4)

(Revelation 7:14)   And I said unto him, Sir, thou knowest. And he said to me, These are they which came out of great tribulation, and have washed their robes, and made them white in the blood of the Lamb.

(Revelation 20:4)   And I saw thrones, and they sat upon them, and judgment was given unto them: and I saw the souls of them that were beheaded for the witness of Jesus, and for the word of God, and which had not worshipped the beast, neither his image, neither had received his mark upon their foreheads, or in their hands; and they lived and reigned with Christ a thousand years.

THIS PHASE THREE (3) OF THE FIRST RESURRECTION IS YOUR OPPORTUNITY TO STILL BE TAKEN

PHASE 3 OF THE FIRST RESURRECTION IS CALLED THE GLEANINGS or The Gathering by The Lord

Jesus Christ of the righteous of, **THE LEFTOVERS** who come out of The Great Tribulation!   Phase 1 & 2 of The First Resurrection have occurred, there is only one phase left!   Though you have been Left Behind!   The Lord God knew that there would be those like you who were a believer but not ready yet to meet Him in the air when He came for His Church in The Rapture! He knew there would be those who missed the mark, or maybe were deceived by the enemy, or would love the world more than they loved God, those who would not be **READY FOR THE HARVEST!** Primarily, God knew **THERE WOULD BE LEFTOVERS!** So, in His infinite wisdom He has allowed for Phase 3 of **The First Resurrection** to give those left behind an opportunity to still make it, if they are willing to face the price that must be paid to gain eternal life!   Because you refused to endure the test of life and secure your transition in The Rapture, now you must be tested with your life in order to inherit the Kingdom of God! **The Gleanings,** to make it plain, refers to deceived believers and maybe even non-believers forced to go through The Great Tribulation who were not included in the main Harvest (The Rapture.).   This final resurrection period is completed at the time of Jesus' return, or Second Coming, at the end of The Great Tribulation!   This means that the duration of Phase 3 of The First Resurrection Period when The Gleanings will be resurrected will be during the entire remaining period of The Great Tribulation after the Rapture of the Church!   So, those left behind will be tested in the most horrific part of the Great Tribulation Period along with the wicked: I will speak more on that testing in more detail later! Now, let me reiterate what has been said, for I need you to clearly understand this! You were left behind in The Rapture, but God has still made a way for you to escape eternal damnation! Because you missed The Rapture you will not escape The Great Tribulation that has come upon the whole world to try everyone that is alive on the planet!   It will be a time like no other time in the history of mankind, for it is the final judgment of Satan, the forces of evil and wicked men, women, boys and girls! The terror and horror of it will be unprecedented, for if the days of it are not shortened, no flesh would survive! For you to still be saved from the second death you will be forced, during The Great Tribulation, to make what may seem to be harsh decisions regarding your allegiance, and regarding your life! The decisions you make will determine the eternal future of your soul (your spirit)! It is during this period that The Lord Jesus Christ will gather out those who are worthy and are able to commit to God. He will glean the earth of The Leftovers if they make the choice to follow Him, knowing they have been left behind!

Jesus' return to the earth at His Second Coming to establish His Millennial Reign is separate from The Rapture, which is when the general harvest occurs. Remember, when Jesus came for His Church He didn't return to earth, but rather meets believers in the sky **(1 Thessalonians 4:17). The Gleanings,** include the resurrection of believers who die during The Great Tribulation!

<u>I BELIEVE THERE WILL BE A SECOND GLEANING DURING THE MILLENIAL REIGN OF CHRIST</u>

I believe there is the possibility of a **SECOND GLEANING** at the end of the **Millennial Reign of Christ** of the righteous who lived in the Millennial Reign period and died before the 1000 years are up!

> *(Isaiah 65:20)* *Never again will there be in it [Jerusalem] an infant who lives but a few days, or <u>an old man who does not live out his years</u>; <u>the one who dies at a hundred will be thought a mere child;</u> <u>the one who fails to reach a hundred</u> will be considered accursed.*

The passage simply shows that at the end of **The Great Tribulation** when Christ sets up His 1000 Millennial Reign and all the righteous ones that were redeemed in all 3 Phases of **The First Resurrection** shall rule with Him! I notice the above scripture that says during His reign, life expectancy will be longer, but people will still die! Lifespans will be greatly increased, as before the flood; but it doesn't say righteous people won't die. In fact, it's implied that blessed people will die by the reference to *an old man who does not live out his years.* Moreover, verse <u>**22 of Isaiah 65**</u> says that God's people will live as long as trees during the Millennium.. Something else to consider: While it's true that many people lived to be over 900 years old before the flood, it's still not a thousand years, which is how as long **The Millennium** will last. Also, some people died well short of 900-plus years; for instance, Lamech died at 777. Someone might argue: How can there be two resurrections or gleanings of the righteous during the Great Tribulation period and another at the end of the Millennium Reign of Christ? Answer: Because the very word gleanings is plural and implies more than one gleaning; after all, the poor gleaned the harvested fields more than once in biblical times. Also, **(Psalm 90:4)** shows that a thousand years is like a day to the LORD, so the two gleanings occur only one day apart from his perspective. The question that I ask myself as the Holy Spirit revealed this possibility to me was: If all the righteous have been gathered during the (3) Phases: **The First Fruits, The Harvest, and The Gleaning**, where did these other righteous humans come from to be gleaned at the end of the Millennial Reign of Christ? The Holy Spirit immediately revealed to me that at the **Second Coming of Jesus Christ**, when He sets up His Kingdom, He will allow the nations lenient to Israel to come into His Kingdom, though they were not saved people! Their support and loving treatment of His Brethren Israel gave them access into the Millennial Kingdom where Christ and the Redeemed Saints will rule for 1000 years!

> **(<u>Matthew 25:34</u>)** *Then shall the King say unto them on His right hand, Come, ye blessed of my Father, inherit the Kingdom prepared for you from the foundation of the world:*

Now understand that the inhabitants of these nations will be unsaved people but will be allowed to live in an utopian world where Christ is King and where Satan and the forces of evil will be bound in the pit for those thousand years!

> *(Revelation 20:3) **And cast him into the bottomless pit, and shut him up, and set a seal upon him, that he should deceive the nations no more, till the thousand years should be fulfilled: and after that he must be loosed a little season.***

Many will accept Christ and be converted or saved, becoming followers of Christ during their lives and many will not! Those that confess Christ, though they die, their bodies will not raise or gleaned to immortality until the end of the 1000 Year Reign of Christ!   It is relevant to say that even these individuals will go through a testing during this time period! Now notice that at the end of the 1000 reign of Christ, Satan and his forces are loosed to temp mankind, loosed to determined who have converted to God or remains in rebellion.

> *(Revelation 20:7-8)   **And when the thousand years are expired, Satan shall be loosed out of his prison! And shall go out to deceive the nations which are in the four quarters of the earth, Gog and Magog, to gather them together to battle: the number of whom is as the sand of the sea. And they went up on the breadth of the earth, and compassed the camp of the saints about, and the beloved city: and fire came down from God out of heaven, and devoured them.***

It is at this time that the Lord Jesus Christ will perform this second Gleaning, gathering the final number of righteous from the wicked, totally purifying the creation of God from sin and wicked ones!   So, I believe that there will be a second gleaning, **BUT IF I WERE YOU AND HAVE BEEN LEFT BEHIND AFTER THE RAPTURE HAS OCCURRED**, I would not depend on this last Gleaning at the end of the 1000 year Reign of Christ; because it is the **<u>Gleaning of the Nations</u>**, and who's to say your nation will have the opportunity to go into the 1000 Reign, that's not guaranteed?   I added this information **<u>NOT FOR YOU TO GAMBLE WITH YOUR ETERNAL FUTURE</u>**, but to let you know how God is intent on gathering all the righteous, even those "unrighteous ones" who became converted during that 1000 Reign, Jesus gleans them before He cast **ALL THE WICKED** into the Lake of Fire!

.

CHAPTER 16
YOU STILL HAVE AN OPPORTUNITY TO MAKE IT TO HEAVEN!

I have given you a lot of information, with the scriptures to back it up, that The Lord Jesus is the Son of God and has all power Heaven and Earth trusted in His hands!   Also, you should know without a doubt that God the Father loves mankind and does not want anyone to perish, but to live eternally with Him!

(2Peter 3:9) The Lord is not slack concerning his promise, as some men count slackness; but is longsuffering to us-ward, not willing that any should perish, but that all should come to repentance.

His promise is of a future judgment, when He will save and gather His people and destroy their enemies! Do not count His longsuffering as slackness; do not impute slackness to Him, because He waits so long before executing His threatened judgments. Yes, He is long-suffering; by waiting so long before He brings destruction on the wicked, He shows His desire that they should repent and be saved. By continuing to show mercy to men and women in life, offering them the Gospel, and beseeching them to embrace it, God shows that He is unwilling that they should perish, and would delight in their repentance and salvation. If the day of the Lord seems delayed, it is not due to slackness. It is rather because God is giving time to call the world to repentance! **Think about it; God sent His only begotten Son to die for you, that's how important you are to Him!**

(2Corinthians 5:21) says: For He hath made Him to be sin for us, who knew no sin; that we might be made the righteousness of God in Him.

God made Jesus to be sin; to suffer to make atonement for our sins and iniquities! Why? That we might be made the righteousness of God; for Christ's sake we can be accepted, and treated as righteous, through faith in Him. God, in giving His Son to die for even His enemies, and in coming by the Gospel through His ministers, and beseeching men to be reconciled to Him, God has shown that He is exceedingly desirous of their salvation; and that if any are lost, it will be because they refuse to be reconciled to Him!

The renewed man acts upon new principles, by new rules, with new ends, and in new company. The believer is created anew; his heart is not merely set right, but a new heart is given to him. He is the workmanship of God, created in Christ Jesus unto good works. Though the same as a man, he is changed in his character and conduct. These words must and do mean more than an outward reformation. The man who formerly saw no beauty in the Savior that he should desire Him, now loves Him above all things. The heart of the unregenerate is filled with enmity against God, and God is justly offended with him. Yet there may be reconciliation. Our offended God has reconciled us to Himself by Jesus Christ. By the inspiration of God, the Scriptures were written, which are the word of reconciliation; showing that peace has been made by the cross, and how we may be interested therein. Though God cannot lose by the quarrel, nor gain by the peace, He beseeches sinners to lay aside their enmity, and accept the salvation He offers. Christ knew no sin. He was made sin; not a sinner, but Sin, a Sin-offering, a Sacrifice for sin. The end and design of all this was, that we might be made the righteousness of God in Him, might be justified freely by the grace of God through the redemption which is in Christ Jesus. Can any lose, labor, or suffer too much for Him, who gave His beloved Son to be the sacrifice for their sins, that they might be made the righteousness of God in Him?

I am asking you today to make a serious choice to come to God and fully accept Jesus and when you accept Jesus, God will accept you! Now re-read Chapter 5 of the Book and make the transaction with God! Please, DO IT NOW!

CHAPTER 17
THIS IS WHAT YOU MUST DO TO BE SAVED FROM THE WRATH TO COME!

I pray and believe that you have revisited **Chapter 5** of this book and received **The Re-Birth** and now you truly are a Child of God. I believe you have been born-again, Praise God! Do not let the enemy play with your mind, all things you receive from God are by faith, just believe! I guarantee you will see a change in yourself, an inner change, not just an outer change, for the outer appeals to the flesh but the inner is of the spirit! So, you have taken the first major step to ensure that you have truly accepted Jesus Christ as your Savior!

So, lets discuss the dilemma that you find yourself in! You are in the middle or beyond of the Great Tribulation Period, a period of seven (7) years and **The Rapture** has taken place, I would guess, in the middle of those 7 years at the 3 ½ year mark! Before we, The Church, were Raptured we were seeing strong signs that The Rapture was close! I am here to warn you that the last 3 ½ years of the Great Tribulation that you are in, are going to be the most horrifying period that the inhabitants of Planet Earth will ever witness! That is because the wrath of God is going to be poured out on the wicked for, He will allow the forces of evil to proceed unrestrained against humanity! This is the time of the judgment of God upon the wicked ones (Satan, the forces of evil, fallen angels, demonic spirits and wicked men and women)! The Anti-Christ will appear, and he will be possessed by Satan himself! The False Prophet is the embodiment of evil that supports and promotes The Anti-Christ! The whole world will be saturated in sin and will be anti-God and anti-Christian! The true Christian Church has been removed along with the Holy Spirit, so sin and evil will be unleashed upon mankind! The world will form a New World Order that will make demands upon all to worship the Anti-Christ (who is Satan) and His image and to receive a mark that will identify you as in allegiance with all who worship the devil over God!

Neither Satan, the forces of evil nor the antichrist are going to tell you that you are submitting your allegiance to Satan; they are deceivers and it doesn't make them any difference how they damn your soul, they will never be truthful. Did Satan tell Adam and Eve that if they disobeyed God, that disobedience would hand Satan the deed to the earth for 6000 years and make Satan the prince of this world with the power of physical death and the ability to bind their spirits in the prison house of hell with no way to escape? No, and he will not tell the world either what he is trying to accomplish by damning their souls with the mark of the beast. During the next 3 ½ years God is going to pour out supernatural judgments upon the inhabitants of planet earth. The whole earth will destabilize, the atmosphere, the oceans, the weather, the earth's rotation; there will be supernatural storms, shifts of the continents, and even the appearances and attacks of supernatural and demonic beings and entities from spiritual dimensions! The pits of hell will be opened and demons that have been confined in chains of darkness will be released upon the planet! So, how will this affect you since you have given you heart to Christ, how will you fit in with the wicked ones? **YOU WILL NOT FIT IN WITH THE WICKED BECAUSE NOW YOUR ALLEGIENCE IS TO THE LORD JESUS CHRIST! BECAUSE YOU DO NOT FIT IN, YOU WILL BE HATED, YOU WILL BE HUNTED, YOU WILL BE IMPRISONED WITH THE SENTENCE OF DEATH UPON YOU! ARE YOU READY FOR THESE THINGS TO HAPPEN? WELL, GET READY, FOR GOD HAS SENT ME TO WARN YOU SO THAT YOU WILL KNOW WHAT TO EXPECT! AND, IF YOU WANT TO ESCAPE THE LAKE OF FIRE, THERE ARE SOME THINGS THAT YOU MUST NOT DO DURING THIS GREAT TRIBULATION PERIOD!** Let's look at some scriptures to clarify your plight:

<u>WARNINGS:</u>

1) **Satan will rule the world through The Anti-Christ and will demand that you worship his image! <u>DO NOT DO IT!</u> You <u>MUST NOT</u> BOW DOWN TO ANY GRAVEN IMAGES OR WORSHP ANYONE BUT CHRIST!**

2) **The Anti-Christ will demand that you receive his mark in order to WORK, BUY, OR SELL! <u>DO NOT DO IT!</u>**

You **MUST NOT** accept THE MARK OF THE BEAST (THEY WILL WANT TO PUT IT IN YOUR RIGHT HAND OR FOREHEAD)!

3) The Anti-Christ will hunt you down for extermination from society! **DO NOT CARE!** MAINTAIN YOUR TRUST IN CHRIST AND HIS WORD, IT SHALL COME TO PAST!!

4) The only way for you to gain eternal life is that you have a tenacity to stand for Jesus Christ! **IT IS YOUR LAST CHANCE!** DO NOT DENY CHRIST, STAND REGARDLESS OF WHAT IT MAY COST YOU!

5) Understand that Satan's Society will martyr all who reject to worship him! **STAND FIRM, & SUFFER FOR CHRIST!**
You **MUST NOT** BE WILLING TO LAY DOWN YOUR LIFE FOR FAITH IN CHRIST!!

6) In order to be saved and receive life eternal with Christ you must be martyred or killed! **BUT YOU WILL LIVE ETERNALLY WITH CHRIST!** ARE YOU WILLING TO DIE? NOW, THAT IS YOUR ONLY WAY TO ETERNAL LIFE IN GLORY!

So, understand what I am saying to you: In order for you to be saved and receive eternal life after being **Left Behind** by Jesus when **The Rapture** took place, now you must be martyred or killed, giving your life for your allegiance to Jesus Christ! It is shameful that this is now your only way into the Kingdom of God, but it is in the Phase (3) of the First Resurrection because you did not live the type of Christian life that would have positioned you to be taken with the true Church in Phase 2 – of The Rapture!

I am telling you, Jesus is coming back to gather **The Gleanings** or the last and leftover saints, like yourself, for you can trust the Word of God.   And the fact that you have, before we started this chapter, received the rebirth (been born-again) sets you up for the favor of God!   When you are martyred, thought your body will die, you spirit will live on and be translated to Heaven and be keep under the altar:

(Revelation 6:9)   **And when he had opened the fifth seal, I saw under the altar the souls of them that were slain for the word of God, and for the testimony which they held:**

John saw under the altar the spirits or souls of them that were slain for the Word of God. These are clearly the Tribulation Christians who had suffered martyrdom! They had died for their trust in the Word of God. They were under the altar in Heaven! Since the temple is typical of the church, the altar, or center of worship), points to the church and its worship. The brazen altar stood at the door of the tabernacle, and at the bottom of it all the blood of the offerings was poured **(Leviticus 4:7).** Their position probably points out that their own blood was poured out for Christ! For they would not worship the beast (Satan) nor bow to his image, nor accept his mark and were slain!

He saw the souls of the martyrs at the feet of Christ.

Persecutors can only kill the body; after that there is no more, they can do; the soul lives. God has provided a good place in the better world, for those who are faithful unto death. It is not their own death, but the sacrifice of Christ, that gives them entrance into heaven. The cause in which they suffered, was for the Word of God; the best any man can lay down his life for is; faith in God's Word, and the unshaken confession of that faith. They commit their cause to Him to whom vengeance belongs. The Lord is the comforter of His afflicted servants, and precious is their blood in His sight. As the measure of the sin of persecutors is filling up this, **THE END OF THE AGE**, so is the number of the persecuted, martyred Servants of Christ. When this is fulfilled, God will send Tribulation to those who trouble them, and unbroken happiness and rest to those that are troubled.

<u>YOU CAN BE CONFIDENT THAT ALL TRIBULATION SAINTS WILL BE GATHERED!</u>

<u>(Revelation 6:10-11)</u> And they cried with a loud voice, saying, How long, O Lord, holy and true, dost thou not judge and avenge our blood on them that dwell on the earth? And white robes were given unto every one of them; and it was said unto them, that they should rest yet for a little season, until their fellow servants also and their brethren, that should be killed as they were, should be fulfilled.

And they, **THE MARTYRED SAINTS FROM THE TRIBULATION** cried with a loud voice unto The Lord, HOW LONG. Their cry denotes that they had suffered long and severely, and they raise a cry for deliverance! **<u>Jesus informed the Souls under the altar</u>** that their number would be complete sometime near the end of **The Great Tribulation.** The souls of them that were slain; the souls of the martyrs in Christ's cause represent a period of severe persecution. These are seen under the altar, which may mean either the altar of burnt-offering in the court before the temple, or the altar of incense in the outer sanctuary. If, the altar of burnt offering is meant, the idea will be that they have been sacrificed on God's altar as victims in His cause, and their blood poured out beneath it. Those who understand the altar of incense, which was the symbol of intercessory prayer, explain their position from their words as recorded in verse **(Revelation 6:10).**

<u>White robes will be given</u>, which an expression of victory and blessedness. Jesus tells all Tribulation Saints to rest yet for a little season; an intimation that the full time for avenging their blood has not yet come, but that more of them must first be added to their numbers. The Apostle John saw the souls of the martyrs under the altar, at the foot of the altar in Heaven, at the feet of Christ.

You must maintain your faith in the Lord Jesus Christ and; believe in His Word (that is why I am giving you understanding as to what is about to happen to you)! You must be strong in the Lord and not submit to the rulership of the Beast or Anti-Christ nor worship his image and receive his mark! You must know that this will happen to you! You will be cast out and persecuted, without the ability to work, buy or sell and you will be hunted down and killed!   But if you hold out to your commitment to Christ, your soul will go under the altar in Heaven waiting for the **Second Coming of Christ** where you will be transformed into your eternal and glorified bodies and ushered into the **Millennial Reign of Christ** to rule with Him for 1000 years and afterward, take you place in the eternal Kingdom of God!

<u>THOSE NOT TAKEN IN RAPTURE STILL HAS A CHANCE</u>

(<u>Revelation 20:4-6</u>) And I saw thrones, and they sat upon them, and judgment was given unto them: and I saw the souls of them that were beheaded for the witness of Jesus, and for the word of God, and which had not worshipped the beast, neither his image, neither had received his mark upon their foreheads, or in their hands; and they lived and reigned with Christ a thousand years. But the rest of the dead lived not again until the thousand years were finished. This is the first resurrection. Blessed and holy is he that hath part in the first resurrection: on such the second death hath no power, but they shall be priests of God and of Christ, and shall reign with him a thousand years.

The above scriptures is a view of the scene after **The Second Coming of Christ when He returns with The Gleanings or Tribulation Saints supporting the thought that** they shall live (given eternal life) and reign with Christ! John saw that those who sat on the thrones reigned with Christ a thousand years. In the last days the mountain of the Lord's house shall be established in the top of the mountains, and shall be exalted above the hills, and all nations shall flow into it. (**Isaiah 2:2**.) Will Christ come visibly to reign in person as an earthly monarch? The personal coming of the Savior is placed by all the sacred writers as the last event before **The Great Judgment Day!** This great epoch is placed after **The Millennial Reign of Christ, and** after the overthrow of Satan in his last conflict. If the Savior, then, during **The Millennial Reign,** is not visibly present upon the earth, how can He reign? Just as He reigns over each Saint now! Those who know the Lord accept Him as King, but in this period *the knowledge of the Lord shall cover the earth as the waters do the channels of the sea (Isaiah 11:9).* All men shall hear and obey the Gospel, and all shall submit to the beneficent Scepter of Christ!

I wish to reinforce to you that the Souls of them that had been beheaded, you who is in the Tribulation, and desire for your soul to be saved from eternal damnation: **shall live and reign with Christ for a thousand years.** Is this a literal resurrection from the grave? I answer decidedly in the negative. The apostle does not say one word about the resurrection of the bodies of the martyrs, nor does he say that he saw the martyrs themselves. He is particular to say that he saw the souls or spirits of the martyrs living and reigning with Christ. They had been put to death in the body, and their souls were unseen upon the earth, their souls or spirits were found under the altar waiting to be transforms and as the Raptured Saints! They will be made alive, that which were dead meaning their bodies, shall be made alive with Christ at the End of The Great Tribulation! It cannot mean that their souls came to life, for they had never ceased to have existence. That as Christ reigns upon the earth during the millennial period by his truth, so the spirits of the martyrs meet their bodies and are changed into immortal bodies, as the rest of the gathered Church to reign with Christ 1000 years!

.

PRAYER:

MY BROTHER OR SISTER THE PRAYERS OF ALL THE SAINTS IN GLORY ARE BEHIND YOU!

(HEBREWS 12:1)
WHEREFORE SEEING YOU ALSO ARE COMPASSED ABOUT WITH SO GREAT A CLOUD OF WITNESSES, LAY ASIDE EVERY WEIGHT AND THE SIN WHICH DOTH SO EASILY BESET YOU, AND RUN WITH PATIENCE THE RACE THAT IS SET BEFORE YOU!

Father God, I come in the mighty name of Jesus and I come right now, in behalf of the Brother or Sister who is reading this prayer! Father I want to thank you and praise you for salvation through Jesus Christ! You said in your Word in John 17:2 that you gave Jesus power over all flesh that He should give eternal life to as many as you have given unto Him! Thank you for bringing this Brother or Sister into the knowledge of your Word that ***THEY DO HAVE AN OPPORTUNITY!!!*** *I come before You praying that a portion of your strength and power be generated upon this Brother or this Sister that will empower them and sustain them through this period of The Great Tribulation! You have promised that if they believe and trust in your Word, unto death, that you will bring them through not only this ordeal but also transport their spirits into the Heavenly realms of Glory! They have read the book and they have received Jesus in the pardon of their sins, now Most Holy Father, bring them home! Bring them into the congregation of the Saints that I and my fellow heirs of Salvation may meet them and rejoice with in Glory having gained the victory – THROUGH CHRIST JESUS! AMEN!*

MORE ABOUT THE AUTHOR

The Endtime Watchman, Pastor Jerome Z. Greene has been an ordained Minister of the Gospel of Jesus Christ for 46 years and a Pastor for the last 26 years! Pastor Greene was practically born in the Church and was, by the will of God, blessed to sit under the leadership of Pastor Reverend Hampton Minor, who was one of the greatest Prophet/Healers of the twentieth century!   God blessed Pastor Greene, from a young age, to witness the power of God in full manifestation!   As he witnessed, as a child, the gifts of the Holy Spirit operating through Rev. Minor to cast out demons, heal the sick, work miracles, and operate in the gift of prophecy and spiritual leadership left a great spiritual impact, upon the life of J.Z. Greene!   It gave him a different perspective about the spiritual reality of God!   Pastor Greene was saved (Born-Again) at a young age and filled with The Holy Spirit! God commissioned Pastor J. Z. Greene as the Endtime Watchman sending him in the spirit of Jeremiah to warn the Saints in this End of the Ages that the End of Time is near!   God has anointed and imparted unto Pastor Jerome Z. Greene advanced spiritual knowledge in the End of Time Prophecies, the deeper truths of God's Word, and the Development of the Saints of God in how to walk in the Faith and in the Spirit!   J.Z. Greene has been anointed with several gifts of the Spirit such as, the Word of Wisdom; the Word of Knowledge; Gifts of Healing; Prophecy; and Discerning of Spirits!
In his secular career Pastor Greene worked at McDonnell-Douglas and the Boeing Company as an Engineer for over 38 years while he was preaching the Gospel of Christ and Pastoring his church assemlby. He holds both Bachelor and Master Degrees in the schools of men!   But he will be the first to tell you that those degrees and educational achievements mean absolutely nothing in the work of the Lord and the spiritual knowledge he's gained regarding The Kingdom of Heaven!
He will let you know, everything he knows about God, the spirit world, the Kingdom of Heaven, and all spiritual and revelation knowledge, he received from **THE SCHOOL OF THE HOLY SPIRIT!**
God instructed JZ to stand on His Word, to preach and teach the Gospel of Christ to all the world, to Release Spiritual Knowledge, which are the deeper truths of God's Word, to unite His people, and warn the Church; The Body of Christ, that Jesus Christ is soon to come, **WILL YOU BE READY!**

www.ingramcontent.com/pod-product-compliance
Lightning Source LLC
Chambersburg PA
CBHW071623030726
47598CB00001B/411